Name ....

Functional Skills
English: Reading
Level 2

Course Booklet

Answers available online

CGP Books — The Choice of <u>Champions</u>!

They know it... you know it... everyone knows it!

cgpbooks.co.uk

Contents

✓ Use the tick boxes to check off the topics you've completed.

About This Booklet .... 1 ☐
Knowledge Organiser .... 2 ☐

Section One — How Ideas Are Presented

Identifying Purpose .... 4 ☐
Identify different styles of writing and writer's voice.

Facts .... 6 ☐
Follow an argument, identifying different points
of view and distinguishing fact from opinion.

Opinions .... 8 ☐
Follow an argument, identifying different points
of view and distinguishing fact from opinion.

Distinguishing Fact from Opinion .... 10 ☐
Follow an argument, identifying different points
of view and distinguishing fact from opinion.

Bias .... 12 ☐
Analyse texts, of different levels of complexity, recognising their
use of vocabulary and identifying levels of formality and bias.

Implied Ideas .... 14 ☐
Identify implicit and inferred meaning in texts.

Inferred Ideas .... 16 ☐
Identify implicit and inferred meaning in texts.

Following an Argument .... 18 ☐
Follow an argument, identifying different points
of view and distinguishing fact from opinion.

Identifying Types of Text .... 20 ☐
Identify different styles of writing and writer's voice.

Organisational Features .... 22 ☐
Understand organisational features and use
them to locate relevant information in a range
of straightforward and complex sources.

Language Features .... 26 ☐
Understand the relationship between textual features
and devices, and how they can be used to shape
meaning for different audiences and purposes.

Identifying Tone .... 30 ☐
Identify different styles of writing and writer's voice.

Identifying Style .... 32 ☐
Identify different styles of writing and writer's voice.

Thinking About Word Choices .... 34 ☐
Identify different styles of writing and writer's voice.

Formality .... 36 ☐
Analyse texts, of different levels of complexity, recognising their
use of vocabulary and identifying levels of formality and bias.

Section Two — Finding Information in Texts

Identifying Points .... 38 ☐
Identify the different situations when the main points are
sufficient and when it is important to have specific details.

Identifying Details .... 40 ☐
Identify the different situations when the main points are
sufficient and when it is important to have specific details.

Spotting Similarities .... 42 ☐
Compare information, ideas and opinions in different
texts, including how they are conveyed.

Spotting Differences .... 44 ☐
Compare information, ideas and opinions in different
texts, including how they are conveyed.

Section Three — Comparisons

Comparing Information and Ideas .... 46 ☐
Compare information, ideas and opinions in different
texts, including how they are conveyed.

Comparing Opinions .... 48 ☐
Compare information, ideas and opinions in different
texts, including how they are conveyed.

How Information is Conveyed .... 50 ☐
Compare information, ideas and opinions in different
texts, including how they are conveyed.

Section Four — Reference Materials

Using Reference Materials .... 52 ☐
Use a range of reference materials and appropriate sources (e.g.
glossaries, legends/keys) for different purposes, including to find
the meanings of words in straightforward and complex sources.

Topic-based Questions

Identifying Information.................................56
Facts, Opinions & Bias...............................58
Organisational Features.............................60
Language Features....................................62
Making Comparisons.................................64

Exam-style Practice

Exam-style Practice..................................66

About the Test...71
Individual Learning Plan............................72
Glossary...74

Unlock your Digital Extras

To get your free digital extras, go to **cgpbooks.co.uk/fs-english** or scan the QR code below.

This will take you to:
- An answer booklet
- More Individual Learning Plan pages
- A Knowledge Retriever

Published by CGP

Written by Claire Lloyd

Reviewer: David Norden

Editors: Aimee Ashurst, Tom Carney, Polly Jackson, Adam Worster

With thanks to Glenn Rogers for the proofreading.
With thanks to Beth Linnane for the copyright research.

Specification points in Contents contain public sector information licensed under the Open Government Licence v3.0. https://www.nationalarchives.gov.uk/doc/open-government-licence/version/3/

ISBN: 978 1 83774 211 0
Printed by Elanders Ltd, Newcastle upon Tyne.
Graphics from Corel®

Text, design, layout and original illustrations © Coordination Group Publications Ltd (CGP) 2025 All rights reserved.

Photocopying this book is not permitted, even if you have a CLA licence.
Extra copies are available from CGP with next day delivery • 0800 1712 712 • www.cgpbooks.co.uk

About This Booklet

This course booklet supports your learning of the 'Reading' part of the Level 2 qualification.

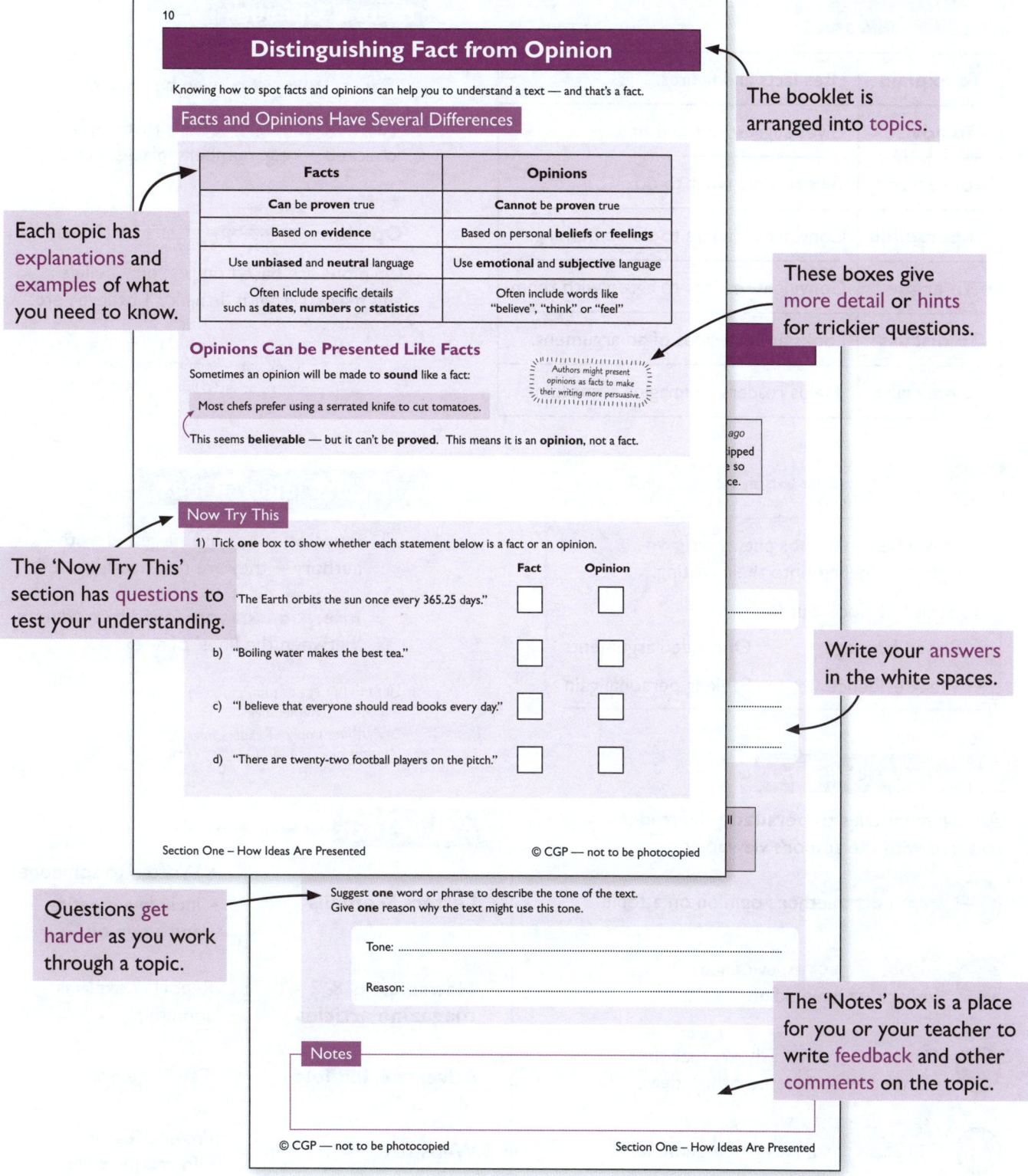

At the end of the booklet, you'll find:
- **Topic-Based Questions**: more practice — all multiple-choice and split into **topics**.
- **Exam-style Practice**: trickier questions that will test you on **every** topic from the booklet.
- **Individual Learning Plan**: to track your progress towards your **learning goals**.

Knowledge Organiser

This Knowledge Organiser has everything you need to know in one place — handy!

Purposes of Texts

To explain	Uses facts and figures.
To advise	Gives suggestions and tips.
To instruct	Tells readers what to do.
To persuade	Convinces readers to do something.
To argue	Convinces readers to agree with them.
To discuss	Looks at both sides of an argument.
To describe	Helps readers to imagine something.

Facts & Opinions

Facts ⟶ Can be proven

Facts include exact details that can be checked — e.g. numbers, places, dates.

Opinions ⟶ Can't be proven

Opinions are based on personal beliefs and may start with 'I think', 'I believe', etc.

Look out — opinions are sometimes presented as facts, but they can't be proved.

Bias

Some texts are more biased than others.

Bias is when an author puts their own opinions or feelings into their writing.

To spot bias, look out for:
- Biased language
- One-sided arguments
- Weak evidence
- Seeking personal gain

Implied & Inferred Ideas

- **Implied ideas** are *suggested* by the author — they are not clearly stated.
- **Inferred ideas** are found by reading 'between the lines' of a text.

Remember: Authors imply. Readers infer.

Following Arguments

An argument tries to **persuade** the reader to agree with the author's viewpoint.

1. Main point: author's opinion on a topic.
2. Supporting points: evidence to back up main point.
3. Counter-argument: shows that the author has considered other ideas.
4. Conclusion: summary of argument.

Types of Text

Letters & emails	⟶	• Written to someone. • Include a greeting and a sign-off.
Newspapers & magazine articles	⟶	Reports / explains something.
Adverts & leaflets	⟶	Catch the eye.
Websites	⟶	Provide & store information online.

Organisational Features

The way a text is organised:
- Headlines
- Subheadings
- Footnotes
- Tables
- Lists

&

The way a text looks:
- Fonts
- Graphics / captions
- Highlighting ⟶ **Bold** / *Italics* / Colour

Knowledge Organiser

Language Features

- **Similes** compare two things using "as" or "like".
- **Metaphors** describe things by saying they're something else.
- **Idioms** have a set meaning different to their literal meaning.

- **Direct address / questions** make the text more **personal**.
- **Rhetorical questions** encourage the reader to **agree**.
- The **rule of three emphasises** a point.
- **Emotive language** appeals to the reader's **feelings**.

Points & Details

The **main point** of a text is its central idea. It's usually found in the first sentence / paragraph. Look for parts of the text that tell you:

Who   What   Where   When   Why   How

Details provide evidence for arguments. They include:

Numbers   Dates   Names

Organisational features like subheadings, tables and graphs can often help you find details.

Tone & Style

Tone can be:
Personal or impersonal
Positive or negative

Style can be:
Explanatory   Advisory
Humorous

These are just some common styles — there are many more.

Formal writing sounds **serious** and is usually used in professional situations.

Informal writing sounds **chatty** and is usually used with friends and family.

Word Choice

- Word choices can affect a text's **meaning** or **tone**.
- The words used in a text should match its **audience**.

Similarities & Differences

Texts can have many similarities and differences. To spot them:

(1) Look at each text:
- What is the main point?
- How much detail is given?
- What type of information is used?
- How is information conveyed?

(2) See where they **agree** or **disagree**.

Making Comparisons

Things you can compare include:

- Key points
- Use of facts
- Styles & tones
- Opinions
- Layouts
- Language features

Use **comparing words** and phrases:

- "Text A is *more / less* ... than Text B."
- "*In contrast to* Text A, Text B ..."

Reference Materials

- You can use a **dictionary** to look up the meaning of a word you don't understand.

Texts might contain **reference materials**:

Table of Contents	Shows what sections of a text are **about**.
Index	Lists **specific** terms.
Glossary	Provides key **definitions**.
Appendix	Gives **extra** information.

Identifying Purpose

All texts have a purpose. For example, the purpose of this course booklet is to help you pass your test.

The Purpose is the Reason a Text Has Been Written

Texts Can Have Many Purposes:

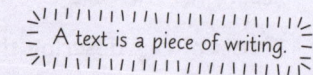
A text is a piece of writing.

Purpose	Example	Common Features
To **Explain** or **Inform**	*Leaflets*	Uses **facts** and **figures** to tell readers about a topic.
To **Advise**	*Guidebooks*	Gives readers **suggestions** or **tips** about something.
To **Instruct**	*Recipes*	Uses **simple language** to tell the reader exactly **what to do**.
To **Persuade**	*Adverts*	Tries to **convince** the reader to **do** something.
To **Argue**	*Complaints*	Tries to make the reader **agree** with a **point of view**.
To **Discuss**	*Comparison*	Examines **both** sides of an **argument** to reach a **conclusion**.
To **Describe**	*Reviews*	Helps readers **imagine** what something is **like**.

A Text Can Have More Than One Purpose

Texts often have **more** than one purpose.
E.g. an advert that informs you about a product and persuades you to buy it.

Now Try This

1) Read the following texts and draw lines to match each one to its main purpose.

> Please come to the barbecue later!
> It's going to be a lot of fun.
> 11:36am

to instruct

The Multown Chronicle LOCAL NEWS
Ten Ways to Reduce Household Waste

to describe

The tall pine trees cast a shadow over the mountainous landscape. Deer stepped carefully across the slowly trickling stream.

to persuade

Identifying Purpose

2) Read the following text.

> ★☆☆☆☆ Without a doubt, the worst café I've ever been to. *7 hrs ago*
> The rudest staff I've ever met. I recommend staying away from this place.

Tick the main purpose of the text from the options below.

☐ To instruct   ☐ To explain   ☐ To advise

3) Read the text below, then answer the questions underneath.

10 FILMS YOU NEED TO WATCH

NUMBER ONE: *Frozen Over*
(2025, directed by Mats Winter)

Frozen Over is the best film of the summer — the last fifty summers, even. If you watch one film this year, make it this one.

To begin with, it's full of excitement. There's a car chase, an avalanche and a terrifying villain who really will give you goosebumps.

What I really love about the film, though, is the music. I am convinced that whoever wrote the soundtrack is a true genius. The sweeping violins, the pounding drums, the haunting vocals... A complete masterpiece.

Frozen Over is available to stream now. For the full list, click *this link*.

Find **two** purposes of this text. Give an example to support each answer.

Purpose 1: ....

Example: ....

Purpose 2: ....

Example: ....

Notes

Facts

You need to know what facts are, what facts look like and why facts are used in texts.

Facts Can be Proved True

You Need to be Able to Spot Facts

- A fact is **objective** ⟶ They are based on evidence, not on personal opinions.
- A fact is **specific** ⟶ They include exact details — such as numbers, dates or places.
- A fact can be **proved** ⟶ They can be checked and confirmed.

Facts Can be Used in Many Ways

- Facts are **informative** ⟶ They provide information about a subject.
- Facts support **arguments** ⟶ They can back up an author's points.
- Facts can be **explanatory** ⟶ They can describe how something works.

Now Try This

1) Read the sentences below.
   Tick the box next to each sentence containing a fact.

   The swimmer thought the pool was a metre too short. ☐

   The indoor pool is exactly 10 metres long. ☐

   They should keep the gym open until 10 pm. ☐

   The new leisure centre opened 6 months ago. ☐

2) Find **two** facts in the text below.

The Amazon Rainforest is the largest tropical rainforest in the world, and it really is a remarkable place. It has captured the hearts and minds of so many people.
The many animal species who call the rainforest home are fascinating.
You can't imagine the variety of life in the forest until you see it with your own eyes.
It is home to over 400 billion trees. Many people think that the trees in the Amazon Rainforest are hugely important, and that we must look after them.

   Fact 1: ....

   Fact 2: ....

Section One – How Ideas Are Presented

Facts

3) Which of the following texts is most likely to contain facts?
Tick **one** box.

An email to a friend about your favourite film. ☐

A review of a new restaurant. ☐

A newspaper report about a natural disaster. ☐

A magazine article about wedding dresses. ☐

4) Read the following text.

> Greetings from the Great Wall of China!
>
> I didn't expect it to be as long as it is — it stretches over 13,000 miles from start to finish. It must have taken hundreds of years to build, if not thousands.
>
> According to our tour guide, it was built to protect China from their enemies. It probably would have scared me off!
>
> It runs from the Bohai Sea to the Gobi Desert. I can't wait to show you the photos I've taken.
>
> *from Preeti.*
>
> Alex Lewis
> 1B New St
> Miltown, Fairshire

a) Write down **three** facts about the Great Wall of China.

Fact 1: ....

Fact 2: ....

Fact 3: ....

b) Suggest **one** way you could prove that these facts are true.

Fact 1: ....

Notes

Section One – How Ideas Are Presented

Opinions

This is the most exciting course booklet that's ever been written — but that's just my opinion.

Opinions Cannot be Proved True

An Opinion is What Someone Thinks

→ Opinions are based on personal **beliefs**, **feelings** or **judgements**.

→ This means that they are **subjective** — they **can't be proved**.

Look Out for Opinionated Writing

- **Subjective language** is anything that presents a **personal** view.
  For example: "I think...", "I believe...", "In my opinion...", "Everyone knows..."
- **Emotive language** uses words that show **strong feelings**.
  For example: "terrible", "wonderful", "best", "ridiculous"
- Opinions don't need to be supported by evidence.

Now Try This

1) Read the following sentences.
   Tick the box next to each sentence containing an opinion.

   Research suggests that global water levels will continue to rise. ☐

   I would argue that this shop is nicer than the other one. ☐

   We all know that walking is more enjoyable than running. ☐

   Scientific studies show that regular exercise is important. ☐

2) Read the following text.
   Underline the **three** opinions that are in the text.

   > **Waste of Time!**
   > Cari Selvon   posted 11:39am.
   >
   > Social media is ruining society. I can't stand how people spend all day on their phones. They could engage in conversations with each other. Scientists have even come up with a smartphone addiction scale. On average, people are spending about 4 hours every day on their phone. If you ask me, we'd all be better off if we spent less time online and more time enjoying the present moment.

   Each opinion is a full sentence.

Section One – How Ideas Are Presented

Opinions

3) Read the following text.

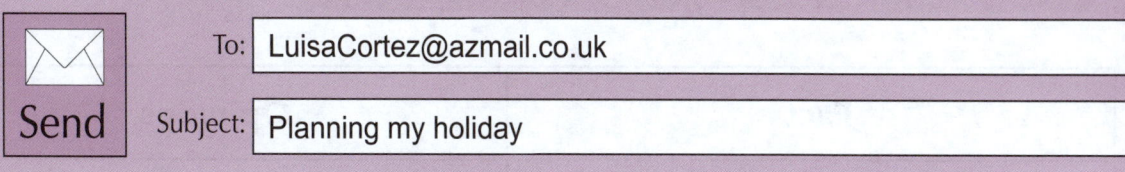

To: LuisaCortez@azmail.co.uk

Subject: Planning my holiday

Dear Luisa,

I can't decide when to go on holiday this year.

    Many people believe that summer is the most enjoyable season. After all, the days are longer and warmer in summertime. However, I think that winter is my favourite. It often snows in winter, and I find it soothing to sit by the fire. Then again, some say spring is the most beautiful time of year, with blooming flowers and milder temperatures. I think the weather is the most important thing to consider when planning a holiday.

    What do you think?

Kind regards,
Ani Norrell.

a) Underline **five** opinions that are in the text.

b) Give **two** examples of **subjective language** in the text.

1: ....

2: ....

c) Give **two** examples of **emotive language** in the text.

1: ....

2: ....

Notes

Distinguishing Fact from Opinion

Knowing how to spot facts and opinions can help you to understand a text — and that's a fact.

Facts and Opinions Have Several Differences

Facts	Opinions
Can be **proven** true	**Cannot** be **proven** true
Based on **evidence**	Based on personal **beliefs** or **feelings**
Use **unbiased** and **neutral** language	Use **emotional** and **subjective** language
Often include specific details such as **dates**, **numbers** or **statistics**	Often include words like "believe", "think" or "feel"

Opinions Can be Presented Like Facts

Sometimes an opinion will be made to **sound** like a fact:

> Most chefs prefer using a serrated knife to cut tomatoes.

This seems **believable** — but it can't be **proved**. This means it is an **opinion**, not a fact.

Authors might present opinions as facts to make their writing more persuasive.

Now Try This

1) Tick **one** box to show whether each statement below is a fact or an opinion.

	Fact	Opinion
a) "The Earth orbits the sun once every 365.25 days."	☐	☐
b) "Boiling water makes the best tea."	☐	☐
c) "I believe that everyone should read books every day."	☐	☐
d) "There are twenty-two football players on the pitch."	☐	☐

Distinguishing Fact from Opinion

2) Decide if each sentence below is a fact or an opinion.
   Give **one** reason to explain your choices.

   a) Social media is extremely harmful to children.

   b) In my view, parents must limit their children's screen time.

   c) Some studies show that holding a screen too close to your face can cause eye strain.

   d) Many smartphones have settings designed to give you more control of your children's screen time.

Sentence	Fact or Opinion?	Reason
a	....	....
b	....	....
c	....	....
d	....	....

3) Read the following text.

HUGE FURNITURE SALE!

Make great savings!

Go to Boughtfield & Co for the best furniture in town.
With free delivery for orders over £100, what's not to love?

- 50% off everything in-store!
- The shop is open from 9 am to 5 pm.
- Plus: an all-new kitchen range you're going to love.

---

a) Circle any facts in the text.

b) Underline any opinions in the text.

Notes

Bias

Bias can sometimes be tricky to spot, but the following pages will give you the practice you need.

Bias is Favouring One Idea Over Others

Bias is when an **author** puts their **own opinions** into their writing.

They might do this to make their opinions seem better than others and **influence** the reader.

There are Several Ways to Spot Bias

- **Language choices.** → Look out for emotive or forceful language.

- **Lack of evidence.** → Statements might not be supported by facts.

- **One-sided.** → Biased arguments may not consider other views.

- **Personal gain.** → Authors might benefit from sharing a certain opinion.

Some Texts are More Biased Than Others

Less Biased	More Biased
"I prefer Milly's Tearoom. The cakes are up to £1 cheaper there than at Bloombird."	"The cakes at Bloombird are the best. I should know — I own the bakery."
<ul><li>Considers two points of view.</li><li>Doesn't use emotional language.</li><li>Uses facts to support opinion.</li><li>Doesn't try to influence readers.</li></ul>	<ul><li>Has just one point of view.</li><li>Uses emotional language.</li><li>Claim isn't supported by evidence.</li><li>Tries to influence readers — the author owns Bloombird Bakery and wants more people to go there.</li></ul>

Now Try This

1) Read the text descriptions below.
   Tick the **two** texts that are most likely to be biased.

   A museum's list of historical births and deaths. ☐

   A book review written by the book's publisher. ☐

   An article about a politician written by their sibling. ☐

   Authors don't always realise their writing is biased.

Bias

2) Read the following text.

> Bus travel is essential. It's environmentally friendly and helps to reduce traffic. Plus, it's much cheaper than owning a car. Running a bus service has shown me just how many people appreciate the need for good, reliable public transport.

a) Is this text biased? Circle your answer.   **Yes / No**

b) Give **one** reason for your answer.

   ....

3) Read the following texts.

Text 1:

> "I have never been more excited."   An Interview with Joey Bridge.
>
> Joey Bridge is surely one of the most talented actors of our time. The people who criticise Joey obviously have no idea what they're talking about. Today I talk to the actor — who is one of my oldest friends — about his successful career on the stage.

Text 2:

> **HEALTH NOTICE**
>
> Carers, make sure that you wash your hands thoroughly when attending to our patients. Bacteria spread more easily on unwashed hands, so please help us to reduce this risk.

a) Which of these texts is biased? Circle your answer.   **Text 1 / Text 2**

b) Give **one** reason for your answer.

   ....

Notes

Implied Ideas

You'll come across implied ideas all the time in your reading — so you need to know all about them.

Implied Ideas are Not Clearly Stated

Implying is Suggesting Things Without Saying Them

- Authors don't always say exactly what they mean.
- They may **imply** what they mean — leaving it up to the **reader** to **figure it out**.

You Need to be Able to Spot Implied Ideas

Pay attention to the **less obvious meanings** and **word choices** in a text.

> Zeinab hums to herself as she steps out into the glorious sunshine.

Zeinab is humming, which suggests that she feels happy.

This is a positive description, which adds to the suggestion that Zeinab feels happy.

Now Try This

1) Read the following messages.

 Jay, you've been to the new Thai restaurant down the street — what did you think of it?

I love Thai food but I don't think I'll be going back.

 Do you think it would be a good place to take my mum when she visits next week?

I think she'd prefer The Sun Inn on Hatley Road.

a) Suggest **one** thing that Jay's message about the Thai restaurant implies.

....

b) Suggest **one** thing that Jay's message about The Sun Inn implies.

....

Implied Ideas

2) Read the following text.

> Looking for the best night's sleep?
> Tired of lying on lumps and bumps?
> **Try our premium memory foam mattress.**
>
> FOAM FANTASTIC!
> Prices start from £199.99

a) Suggest **one** thing that the text implies about Foam Fantastic's mattresses.

....

b) What does the text imply about other companies' mattresses? Tick **one** box.

They are better than Foam Fantastic's mattresses. ☐

They are the same as Foam Fantastic's mattresses. ☐

They are worse than Foam Fantastic's mattresses. ☐

c) Give **one** reason for your answer to part (b).

....

3) Read the following text.

> Mark is a brilliant student and I think he'll go far in whatever career he picks.
> However, he regularly misses the deadlines for his coursework assignments.
> Despite this, the work he does hand in on time is an absolute joy to read.

a) Give **one positive** thing that the author implies about Mark.

....

b) Give **one negative** thing that the author implies about Mark.

....

Notes

Inferred Ideas

Imagine yourself as a detective, pulling out a magnifying glass to find hidden clues — that's inference.

Inferring Means Reading Between the Lines

Inference Can Involve Guesswork

Readers can use **evidence** in a text to make an **educated guess** — this is an **inference**.
Your inference might also use some of your **own knowledge** about a topic.

| The dog started barking as soon as he saw Harvey arrive. | You might infer that the dog is excited. Dogs sometimes bark to greet people. |

Authors imply things, and it's up to the reader to infer them.

Different People Can Make Different Inferences

Many texts can be read in **more than one way**.
Any inference that you make needs to be supported by evidence from the text.

| The dog started barking as soon as he saw Harvey arrive. | You might infer that the dog is nervous. Dogs sometimes bark when they feel afraid. |

Now Try This

1) Read the following text.

> **Victory for the Townspeople** 3h ago
>
> The new car park on Melbrow Road has opened and everyone is delighted. No more will it be a mad rush for spaces on the high street — instead, a smooth, painless journey into the perfectly designed Melbrow car park awaits. Residents are already signing up for the generously discounted parking permit.

   a) How do you think the author feels about the new car park?
      Tick **one** box.

      Annoyed ☐   Nervous ☐   Pleased ☐

   b) Give **one** word or phrase from the text that supports your answer to part (a).

      ....

Section One – How Ideas Are Presented

Inferred Ideas

2) Read the following text.

> The teacher handed back the test papers to her students. Orlaith's face lit up as soon as she saw her score, but Iain buried his head in his hands and tossed the paper aside.

a) How do you think Iain performed in the test?

....

b) Give **one** reason that supports your answer to part (a).

....

3) Read the following text.

> Jenny looked at her phone and sighed. The clock on the wall seemed to move slower with each passing minute. Across the café, a couple laughed together, completely unaware of Jenny's frown growing larger and larger.

a) Suggest **one** emotion that Jenny might be feeling.

....

b) Give **one** reason for your answer to part (a).

....

c) Give **one** reason Jenny might be checking her phone.

....

Notes

Following an Argument

Don't worry — nobody's going to start shouting. These arguments are for reading purposes only.

An Argument Presents a Viewpoint

Arguments Have a Purpose

- A text's **argument** is **how** the author **presents** their **point of view** on something.
- The **purpose** of an argument is usually to **convince** readers to **agree** with the author.

Arguments Often Use Certain Features

Feature	Description
Main Argument	This is the author's **point of view** on a topic. Usually appears at the **start** of a text.
Supporting points	**Evidence** that backs up the main argument.
Counter-arguments	**Opposing** views that go **against** the main argument. Show that the author has thought about **other opinions**.
Conclusion	The **end** of a text, where the author **summarises** their argument. The main argument might be repeated one last time.

Now Try This

1) Read the following text.

> More people who want a pet should adopt one from a shelter. You can feel that you've really made a difference in your pet's life. Some people think that pets from shelters are difficult, but I've seen plenty of puppies who are terribly behaved.

a) "Some people think that pets from shelters are difficult". What part of an argument is demonstrated in this quotation? Tick **one** box.

Supporting point ☐   Counter-argument ☐

b) What is the main argument of the text?

....

Section One – How Ideas Are Presented

Following an Argument

2) Read the following text.

> **A Four-Day Work Week — Good or Bad?**
> Some studies suggest that a four-day work week would provide employees with more energy and help them balance their work and personal lives better. The benefits are clear — workers would be happier and more productive.
>
> Other studies suggest that a four-day work week would negatively affect the health and hospitality industries, which need to stay open for more than four days a week. More flexible work schedules for employees could help with this.
>
> In conclusion, the personal benefits of a four-day work week seem to outweigh the costs to businesses, and companies should give it serious consideration.

a) What is the main argument of the text?
Tick **one** box.

- Companies should avoid changes to the working week. ☐
- A four-day work week would improve employees' lives. ☐
- Employees prefer working fewer hours. ☐

b) Which of the following is a supporting point given by the author?
Tick **one** box.

- A greater work-life balance boosts employees' moods. ☐
- A four-day work week would increase workers' pay. ☐
- Employees like the idea of flexible work schedules. ☐

c) Which of the following is a counter-argument given by the author?
Tick **one** box.

- Some industries can't be flexible with their opening hours. ☐
- Employees are less productive when they work fewer hours. ☐
- Four-day work weeks are less expensive for businesses. ☐

Notes

Identifying Types of Text

You'll see a range of texts in your exam — these pages look at some of the types you need to know.

Different Texts Have Different Jobs

Recognising Different Texts

All texts are different, but some types of text are more likely to use certain features.

Type of Text	Features
Letters and emails	• Written to somebody. • Have a **greeting** and a **sign-off**. • Include a home **address** or an email **address**.
Newspaper and magazine articles	• Used to **report** or **explain** something. • Have **headlines** to tell you what they are about. • Use **subheadings** and **columns**.
Adverts and leaflets	• Use bright **colours** and eye-catching **images**. • Use different **fonts** and text sizes to stand out.
Websites	• Used to **provide** and **store** information online. • Often have a **search box** and **links** to other pages. • Sometimes have an **address bar** at the top.

Now Try This

1) Draw a line to link each of the following text types to **one** of their features.

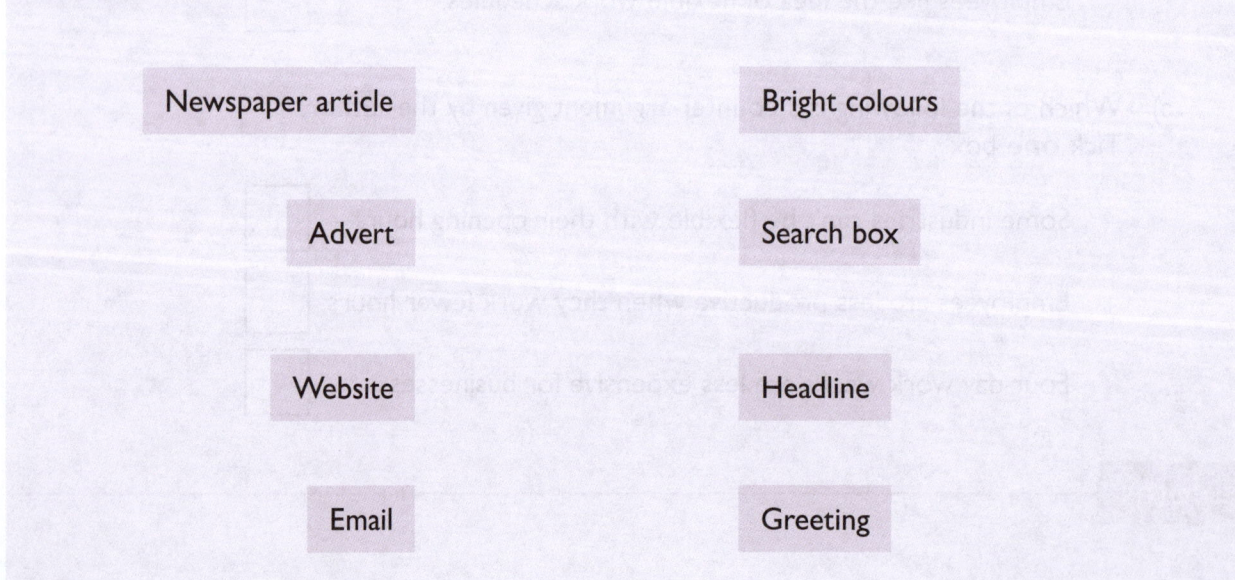

Newspaper article   Bright colours

Advert   Search box

Website   Headline

Email   Greeting

Section One – How Ideas Are Presented

Identifying Types of Text

2) Look at the following text.

   a) What type of text is this?

   ....

   b) Name **one** feature that tells you this.

   ....

3) Look at the following text.

   a) What type of text is this?

   ....

   b) Name **two** features that tell you this.

   Feature 1: ....

   Feature 2: ....

Notes

Organisational Features

It's not just the words of a text you have to look at — think about how texts are arranged, too.

A Text is More Than Words on a Page

The way a text is laid out — its **organisational features** — influences how you read it.

> Organisational features are also called 'presentational features'.

A) Painting Found in Shed

A curious discovery
Earlier this year, school teacher Mr. Lowe decided to clear out his shed. Behind a box he found a painting of a seaside town he had never seen before.

B) "I couldn't believe it!"
His children urged him to take the painting to an expert to get it valued. Mr. Lowe was shocked when he did. He was told it was worth thousands[1].

The mystery remains
Mr. Lowe is still uncertain of how the painting came to be in his shed. "I don't ever plan to sell it," he said.

D) (graphic)
E) The painting, thought to date from the 1810s.

C) [1]Garth Art Advisory gave Mr. Lowe an estimated value of £9,600.

Feature	Where it is Found	Purpose
A) Headlines	At the **top** of the page, usually in a **larger** font.	To grab the reader's **attention**. Tells the reader what a text is **about**.
B) Subheadings	At the **start** of a **section** of text.	To tell the reader what a **section** of a text is **about**.
C) Footnotes	**Beneath** a text. Linked to the text by a number or symbol.	To add **extra** information without interrupting a text.
D) Graphics	May be **anywhere** in a text.	To **show** what a text is about. May be a picture, diagram or chart.
E) Captions	Always appear with a **graphic**.	To **explain** what a graphic is showing.

Now Try This

1) Look at the following part of a text.

> **Town Council Warns of Flood Risk**
> This week, the Ordenton Council have warned local residents of the possibility of severe flooding in the coming days...

Identify the organisational feature shown in this text.
Tick **one** box.

Footnote ☐   Caption ☐   Headline ☐

Organisational Features

2) Look at the text below.

> **Corgan Chocolate** est. 1878 — A
>
> HOME | **The History of Corgan Chocolate**
> ABOUT | **Humble beginnings** ← B
> HISTORY | The Corgan family has long been associated with the making of chocolate. The company was founded in 1878 by Wilfred John Corgan, an innkeeper in Milshire. He got the idea to start selling...

a) Name organisational features **A** and **B**.

A: ....   B: ....

b) Name **one other** organisational feature used in the text.

....

3) Look at the text below.

> **A Note on the Damage to the Library Roof**
>
> The damage to the library roof is extensive and will require serious structural repairs[1]. Charles Lambert wrote to the mayor last week to ask if any further efforts were being made to fix the roof. So far, he has not received a reply.
>
> [1] The full report on the damage to the library roof is on the council website.

a) Name **two** organisational features that the text uses.

1: ....   2: ....

b) Choose **one** of your answers to part (a) and give **one reason** why it is effective.

....

Notes

Organisational Features

As you'll see in *this sentence*, the way **a text looks** can have an effect on HOW YOU READ IT.

A Text Has Visible Features

It's not just about what a text **tells you** — the way it **looks** matters too.

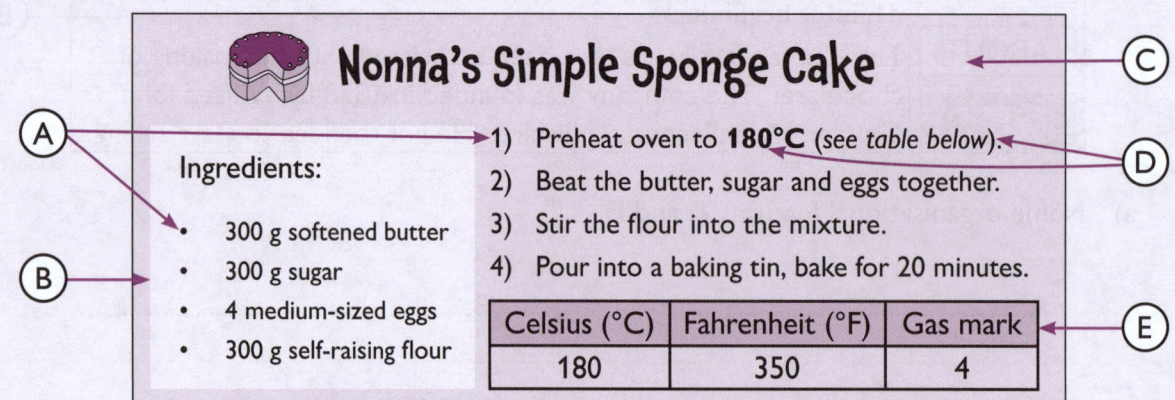

Feature	What it Looks Like	Purpose
A) Lists	**Bullet** points or **numbered** lists.	To **break up** or **order** information.
B) Text boxes	**Separate boxes** within the main text.	To make information **stand out**.
C) Font	How text looks on a page. E.g. **Cartoonish** or **serious**	To help set the **tone** of a text.
D) Highlighting	**Bold**, *italics*, colour.	To **emphasise** parts of a text.
E) Tables	**Rows** and **columns** of information. *You're reading a table now.*	To **organise** information clearly.

Now Try This

1) Read the following text.

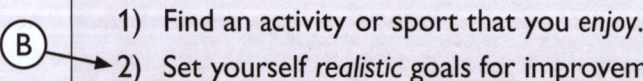

a) Name organisational features **A** and **B**.

A: ....

B: ....

Organisational Features

2) Look at the following text.

> 🍦 **You're invited!** 🍦
> Dear friend,
> Please join us at Yana's 8th birthday party.
> It is at the **Town Hall** on the **17th June**.
> We hope to see you there!
>
> • Drop-off at *10am*.
> • Pick-up at *2pm*.
> *Please don't bring any food containing nuts.*

(A points to "You're invited!" and to "17th June")
(B points to the shaded box with the nuts warning)

a) Name organisational features **A** and **B**.

A: ....   B: ....

b) Choose **one** of your answers to part (a) and give **one reason** why it is effective.

....

3) Look at the following text.

> **Standington Community Theatre — Weekly News**
>
> **Spotlight on: Aya Garten**
> Aya has been involved in a huge number of projects, including:
> 1) Our first ever pantomime!
> 2) Repainting the lobby walls.
> 3) Raising funds for the theatre.
>
> **What's on this month?**
>
> | Variety Show | 8th - 16th Nov |
> | Macbeth | 5th - 23rd Nov |
> | Pantomime | 18th - 24th Dec |

a) Identify **two** organisational features in this text.

Feature 1: ....   Feature 2: ....

b) Give **one** reason why each feature you chose is effective.

Feature 1: ....

Feature 2: ....

Notes

Language Features

Language features are a big part of what makes reading fun — and they can help you understand a text.

Language Features Help a Text Achieve Its Purpose

Authors use language features to have an **effect** on the reader.
They can also use them to make their texts more **interesting** for readers.

Some Language Features Help the Reader's Imagination

Feature	What it is	Example
Simile	A **comparison** of two things using "as" or "like".	Her smile was like sunshine.
Metaphor	A **description** of one thing by saying it **is** something else.	There was a sea of people ahead.
Idiom	A phrase with a **set** meaning that is **different** to its **literal** meaning.	The leaking roof was the tip of the iceberg.

Alliteration Makes a Phrase Memorable

Alliteration is when words that are **close together** begin with the **same sound**.

The wind whistled. — Both of these words start with a 'w' sound.

It is often used to make short, catchy **slogans** for adverts.

Now Try This

1) Read the following sentences.
   Tick **one** box to show whether each sentence is a metaphor or a simile.

	Metaphor	Simile
a) "The parcel was as heavy as an elephant."	☐	☐
b) "The roadworks around here are a nightmare."	☐	☐
c) "The new carpet was as white as snow."	☐	☐
d) "The music rushed from the speakers like a river."	☐	☐

Section One – How Ideas Are Presented

Language Features

2) Read the following text.

> "My Week in Michoacán." 12,547 views
> Last month I spent a week travelling around what I consider to be the jewel of Mexico. My time in Michoacán was like the luxurious landscape there — full of life and colour. The people I met on my trip really went the extra mile to make me feel welcomed.

   a) Give **one** example of alliteration from the text.

   ....

   b) Give **one** example of an idiom from the text.

   ....

3) Read the following text.

> *The Sunday Soprano*: A Review
> Ali Orlin's first album has hit the charts like a cannonball. Orlin is known as "the woman with lightning bolts for hands" — and for good reason. Her talent towers over her rivals. This album will have you on the edge of your seat!

   a) "Ali Orlin's first album has hit the charts like a cannonball" is an example of:

   An idiom ☐   A simile ☐   Alliteration ☐

   b) Name **one other** language feature used in the text. Give **one** example of that feature.

   Feature: ....

   Example: ....

   c) Give **one** reason why the language feature you named in part (b) is effective.

   ....

Notes

Section One – How Ideas Are Presented

Language Features

One good thing about language features is that there's usually plenty in a text for you to spot.

Language Features Can be Persuasive

Language Features Get the Reader Involved

Some authors don't just want to **entertain** their readers.
They may want to **persuade** the reader to take action — e.g. to buy a product or join a group.

Feature	What it is	Purpose	Example
Direct address	Text that refers **directly** to the reader.	Makes the text feel more **personal**.	*You are going to love this book.*
Rhetorical questions	Questions that **don't need an answer**.	Encourages the reader to **agree**.	*Can anybody resist the scent of fresh bread?*
Direct questions	Questions that the **reader** is expected to **answer**.	Makes the reader feel **involved**.	*Have you ever wanted to learn about tennis?*
Rule of three	A **list** of **three** words or phrases.	**Emphasises** the author's point.	*The room was dark, cold and damp.*
Emotive language	**Describing** words that suggest **emotion**.	Appeals to the reader's **feelings**.	*He let out a heartbreaking sob.*

Now Try This

1) Read the following text.

> **Clever Clean**
> cleverclean@azmail.co.uk
> *"Friendly and reliable. Great service."*
> — one thrilled Clever Clean customer.
> Do you want your house to sparkle? Let Clever Clean do the work!

a) Tick the **two** persuasive techniques that are used in this text.

Rule of three ☐   Emotive language ☐   Direct question ☐

b) Give **one** example from the text of each technique.

Feature 1: ....

Feature 2: ....

Language Features

2) Read the following text.

>  **Can you reduce plastic pollution?**
>
> Every year, our oceans are threatened by millions of tonnes of plastic. Just think of all the helpless underwater creatures, now under threat.
>
> Is there anything more important than saving our planet? You know the answer.
>
> We need your voice, your action and your commitment. Don't wait — act now!

a) Give **one** example of a command from the text.

A command tells you to do something.

....

b) Give **one** example of a rhetorical question from the text.

....

c) "We need your voice, your action and your commitment."
Name the **two** language features used in this sentence.

Feature 1: ....   Feature 2: ....

d) Give **one** effect that the heading of the text might have on the reader.

....

e) Give **one** example of emotive language from the text.
Describe the effect this example has on the reader.

Example: ....

Effect: ....

Notes

Identifying Tone

Maybe you can tell that I'm absolutely delighted to tell you all about identifying the tone of a text!

The Tone is the Mood of a Text

Tone is the way an author's **feelings** about a subject come through in their **texts**. Texts can have more than one tone — these pages look at some common ones.

A Tone Can be Personal or Impersonal

- **Personal** writing often contains opinions and may address the reader.
- **Impersonal** writing is usually professional, neutral and factual.

Personal writing might reveal the author's personality, but impersonal writing won't.

A Tone Can be Positive or Negative

- **Positive** writing usually uses more pleasant language.
  Examples of words that convey a positive tone include: 'happy', 'excited' and 'hopeful'.
- **Negative** writing may use less cheerful language.
  Examples of words that convey a negative tone include: 'sad', 'angry' and 'frightened'.

Read Texts Carefully to Identify the Tone

Word choice ➡ Do the words seem professional / friendly / happy / angry?

Sentences ➡ Are sentences long and full of information or short and chatty?

Punctuation ➡ Does the text use lots of exclamation marks?

Context ➡ Who is the text for? Why has it been written?

Now Try This

1) Draw lines to match each sentence below to the correct tone.

Sentence	Tone
The final report will be reviewed on Friday.	Negative
That's brilliant news: I'm thrilled for you!	Excited
The hopeless staff were overrun by rude customers.	Positive
Next week, they'll be staying in a lovely cottage.	Impersonal

Section One – How Ideas Are Presented

Identifying Tone

2) Read the following text.

> ★★★★☆ **Rolling Fields Ranch**　　posted 3 weeks ago
> I loved my stay at Rolling Fields. If you want to wake up to the sight of snow-tipped mountains and grazing cattle, this is where you should go. All of the staff were so kind and the food was excellent. You won't regret a visit to this wonderful place.

a) Is the tone of this text personal or impersonal?

　　Personal ☐　　　Impersonal ☐

b) Give **one** reason for your answer to part (a).

　　...

c) Suggest **one other** word or phrase to describe the tone of this text.
　Give **one** reason for your choice.

　　Tone: ....

　　Reason: ....

3) Read the following text.

> 🔔 **Notice to employees**: Next week's annual department lunch will take place at Vesuvio Tavern at 7:15 pm Please arrive on time.
> If you have any problems, contact management and they will respond quickly.

Suggest **one** word or phrase to describe the tone of the text.
Give **one** reason why the text might use this tone.

　　Tone: ....

　　Reason: ....

Notes

Identifying Style

An author's style will depend on the type of text they're writing, and what their purpose is.

Style is the Way an Author Writes

An Explanatory Style Tells Readers About Something

Explanatory texts use **technical** and **impersonal** language and don't usually include opinions.

> Mass deforestation has gathered concern in the scientific community.

An Advisory Style Tells Readers What to Do

Advisory texts use **clear** and **simple** language which is easy to understand.

> Turn left after the traffic lights, then continue for 100 metres down the road.

Advisory texts often include command words telling you what to do.

A Humorous Style Entertains Readers

Humorous texts may include **exaggeration**, **repetition** and **informal** language.

> I must've dropped a billion plates — I was a really, really rubbish waiter.

Humour can be used to persuade readers.

Now Try This

1) Read the following text.

> *How to switch on your Laser Printer Model x33pc20*
> First, make sure your printer is plugged in with the power cable.
> Next, press the "Power On" button (⏻).
> The button should flash twice before the printer switches on.

a) What type of writing style is this? Circle **one** option.

   Humorous   /   Explanatory   /   Advisory

b) Draw a line to match the following examples from the text to the type of feature they are.

   Next, press   Clear title

   (⏻)   Helpful graphic

   How to switch on your Laser
   Printer Model x33pc20   Command word

Section One – How Ideas Are Presented

Identifying Style

2) Read the following text.

>
> **"Well, Yes!": The Worst Romantic Comedy of The Millennium?**
> This film is so boring it makes watching paint dry seem exciting.
> The plot? Dull. The characters? Dull. The writing? Dull!
> It's the first time I've come out of a cinema wishing I'd just done my laundry instead, which tells you all you need to know about the film.

a) What type of writing style is this? Circle **one** option.

    Humorous   /   Explanatory   /   Advisory

b) Name **one** feature that tells you this. Give **one** example of this feature from the text.

Feature: ....

Example: ....

3) Read the following text.

> **WHAT TO READ?**
> **"Waters of the Nile": A Portrait of Time**
> Eimear Hanulty's new book traces historical trading routes across the River Nile, guiding readers through two hundred years of history. Already, the book has been nominated for three major literary prizes.

a) What type of writing style is this? Circle **one** option.

    Humorous   /   Explanatory   /   Advisory

b) Name **two** features that tell you this.

1: ....   2: ....

c) Suggest **one** reason why the text might use this style.

....

Notes

Thinking About Word Choices

Understanding why an author has chosen certain words can help you to understand a text as a whole.

Word Choices Affect Meaning

Using Specific Words Can Improve Accuracy

- Sometimes a text needs to use more **specific** or **precise** words.
- More specific language usually has a **stronger effect** on the reader.

> Shoe company gives money to charity.

This only gives a general idea.

> Dolney's donates 1.2 million to cancer research.

These words give a more specific idea.

Word Choices Can Influence a Text's Tone

See pages 30-31 for more information on tone.

Words with **similar** meanings can make sentences sound or feel **different**.

> The streets were bustling with shoppers.

This word has a positive tone that suggests a happy and energetic crowd.

> The streets were crowded with shoppers.

This word has a negative tone that suggests the crowd is uncomfortable and tightly-packed.

Choose Words that Suit Your Audience

See pages 36-37 for more information on formality

- **Professional** texts should use **more** formal vocabulary.
- More **casual** or friendly texts can use a **less** formal vocabulary.

Now Try This

1) Tick **one** box to show whether each sentence uses **specific** or **general** words.

	Specific	General
a) "The shop has been closed for a while."	☐	☐
b) "My grandson is a Nurse Practitioner."	☐	☐
c) "It took two hours for traffic to move one mile."	☐	☐
d) "We're running behind on the project."	☐	☐

Thinking About Word Choices

2) Read the following sentences.
   For each sentence, **underline one** word that helps create the tone or style in **bold**.

   a) **Negative**   "The walls had been painted a sickly yellow colour."

   b) **Angry**   "The taxi was ridiculously late to pick us up."

   c) **Formal**   "Do you need any assistance?"

   d) **Specific**   "The furniture was made of recycled plastic."

3) Read the following texts.

Text A:

> Subject: Summer Party
>
> Hey,
> I can't make the summer party, but I'll definitely be at next week's barbecue. See you there — we can hang out.
> All the best,
> Gill.

Text B:

> Subject: Summer Party
>
> Dear Louise,
> I will not be able to attend this year's summer party. I have to participate in a conference that week.
> Regards,
> Gill.

a) Which of these emails would be appropriate to send to a manager at work?
   Tick **one** option.

   Text A ☐   Text B ☐

b) Give **two** words or phrases from that email to support your answer to part (a).

   Word 1: ....   Word 2: ....

c) Give **two** words or phrases from the **other** email that would make it inappropriate to send to a manager.

   Word 1: ....   Word 2: ....

d) Suggest **one** person that it would be appropriate to send the other email to.

   ....

Notes

Formality

These pages will formally introduce you to the differences between a formal and an informal style.

Formality Depends on Context

Formal texts sound serious.
A formal style is mostly used in **professional** contexts — *e.g. reports and job applications.*

Informal texts sound chatty.
An informal style is mostly used in **personal** contexts — *e.g. messages to friends and family.*

You Need to Recognise Formal and Informal Texts

Feature	Formal Writing	Informal Writing
Sentence Structure	**Complete**, often complex sentences.	**Short**, simple sentences.
Tone	**Impersonal** and **professional**.	**Friendly** and **casual**.
Vocabulary	**Precise**, sometimes **technical** language.	**Chatty** language and **slang**.
Contractions	**Rarely** used.	**Frequently** used.

Now Try This

1) Read the following sentences.
   Tick **one** box to show whether each sentence is formal or informal.

                                                                            Formal   Informal

   a) "Thank you for your prompt response to my query." ☐ ☐

   b) "I am writing to confirm my attendance." ☐ ☐

   c) "Hey, when's the next meeting going to be?" ☐ ☐

   d) "Give me a shout when you're at the airport." ☐ ☐

   e) "The conference will take place in March." ☐ ☐

Section One – How Ideas Are Presented

Formality

2) Read the following text.

> 💋 **Auntie Glam** — *our weekly advice column*   ♡ 💻 ↗
> If you're after a new perfume, don't worry. Auntie Glam's here to help!
> I've been wearing *Mighty Fine* all summer and it's a smash hit with my friends.
> It's got a real dab of sophistication about it. Plus, it's on sale at the moment.

a) Is the style of this text formal or informal? Tick **one** box.

Formal ☐   Informal ☐

b) How can you tell?

....

3) Read the following texts.

Text A:

✉ Subject: Chat about feedback.

Hi Amir,
Just checking you're okay with the meeting being moved to tomorrow? Pop into my office when you're here.
Best,
Professor Kaufmann.

Text B:

✉ Subject: Application Update

Dear Ms. Brodie,
Your application to our educational programme has been successful. Please respond swiftly to confirm your place on the course.
Bell Tower Community College.

a) Identify which text is formal and which text is informal.

Formal: ....   Informal: ....

b) Give **one** example of technical language from the formal text.

....

c) Give **one** example of chatty language from the informal text.

....

Notes

Identifying Points

A text can have many points, but there'll usually be a main point — that's the most important one.

Main Points Often Appear First

The main point of a text is its **central idea**, or its most **important information**. This important information is usually in the **first** sentence or paragraph.

Some Questions Only Ask About the Main Point

You don't have to read the **whole** text to answer questions that ask about **one** point. Read the question **carefully** so you know how much detail your answer needs.

Scan for Key Words in the Text

Look for words in the text that tell you any of these things:

1) **Who** is involved.
2) **What** is happening.
3) **Where** it is happening.
4) **When** it is happening.
5) **Why** it is happening.
6) **How** it happens.

It can be helpful to underline key words as you read a text. If you're taking the test on a computer, there is usually a facility to highlight or underline words in the text.

① ② ③ ④

An **escaped lemur** was finally **captured** at **Dittingworth Zoo** this **morning**. **Employees** at the zoo have admitted to **leaving the enclosure gate open**. ⑤ They lured the **escaped lemur** back inside **using its favourite food**.

⑥

Look out for repeated phrases and words as well.

Now Try This

1) Read the following text.

>   **ICY ROAD CONDITIONS**
>
> Freezing temperatures in the local area have caused icy road conditions. Currently, Bakerley Road and Courtney Street are closed to all vehicles. Please be cautious when driving — drive slowly, drive safely, drive sensibly. Conditions are expected to improve towards the end of the week.

What is the main point of this text? Tick **one** box.

The local roads are icy. ☐

It is dangerous to drive in cold weather. ☐

Two streets have been closed. ☐

Identifying Points

2) Read the following text.

> **NOTICE — Local House Wanted for Film Set**
>
> Early next spring, a period drama is due to be filmed in Pendlebrook. The production crew are looking for an appropriate house to use as a set. It needs to have a wide entrance (3 metres) so we can get the set furniture inside. It should look Georgian and have large windows. We also require a sizeable garden. Filming would take no longer than sixteen weeks.

   a) What is the main point of this text? Tick **one** box.

   - [ ] A period drama is going to be filmed in Pendlebrook.
   - [ ] The filming in Pendlebrook will take a long time.
   - [ ] The production crew are trying to find a set for their film.

   b) According to the text, when will the period drama be filmed?

   ....

3) Read the following text.

> Baden-Württemberg is a great region of Germany to visit if you're interested in architecture. There are also some amazing castles and palaces there, including Heidelberg Castle, which hosts spectacular firework displays.
>
> The historic and hilly city of Stuttgart contains some particularly interesting car museums that are worth a look. It is also home to beautiful vineyards!

   a) According to the text, what is **one** reason to visit Baden-Württemberg?

   ....

   b) According to the text, what is the landscape of Stuttgart like?

   ....

Notes

Identifying Details

Paying attention to the more specific details of a text can help you to understand it better.

Some Texts Include Specific Details

Specific Details Can Make a Text More Useful

- Specific details can provide **evidence** that **supports arguments**.
- **Instructions** and **reports** often include specific details to be as **accurate** as possible.

Use Layout Features to Find Details

Organisational features can **guide** you to a text's important details.

- Titles and subheadings tell you **where** the information is.
- **Bold**, *italic* and coloured text highlight key points.
- Tables, graphs and charts **organise** information clearly.

See pages 22-25 for more on organisational features.

Keep an Eye Out for These Details

- Numbers and dates ⟶ "20% of customers", "15 °C", "£1 million", "17th July"
- The names of things ⟶ "Dr. Kaczka", "Pendle Street", "Frank's Florals"

You should also look out for phrases that introduce specific details, for example: "Studies say…" or "The data shows…"

Now Try This

1) Read the following text.

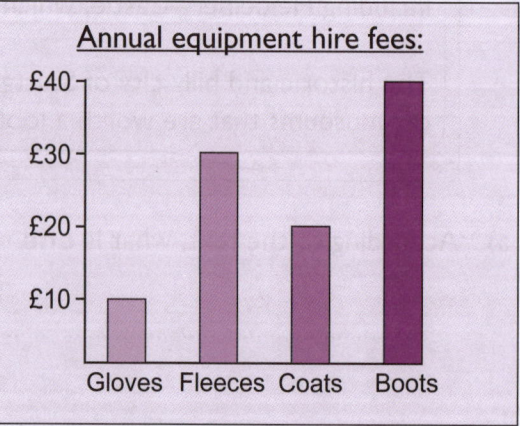

Rothmerton Ramblers' Club

The RRC is a dedicated rambling group, established in 2007. Since then, the group have completed over 400 walks. We have roughly 65 members.

We go for a walk every two weeks, with a monthly meeting in town to plan our routes and socialise. Memberships are £10 a month and can be bought on a monthly or annual basis.

a) How many members does the Rothmerton Ramblers' Club have? Tick **one** box.

Fewer than 60 ☐   Over 60 ☐   Over 70 ☐

b) How much does it cost to hire each of the following pieces of equipment for a year?

Boots: ....   Gloves: ....

Identifying Details

2) Read the following text.

Customer Service Notice

Hay's Tea have started a loyalty card scheme for customers in Penshire. Buying their teabags from participating shops can earn you rewards.

The scheme will run for **one year from 18th May**. Buying **one box** of Hay's Tea earns you **1 point**.

Earn rewards at these shops:
- Agney & Co
- Schorer's
- Eirman Health Foods

Points	Reward	Reward RRP
25	Teapot	£35
50	Tea set	£75
75	Tea Hamper	£110
100	Factory visit	£150

a) Name **two** shops that are participating in the Hay's Tea loyalty card scheme.

1: .... 2: ....

b) Name the layout feature used to present the possible rewards.

....

c) How long is the loyalty card scheme running for?

....

d) How many points are needed to earn the tea set?

....

e) What is the RRP of the tea hamper?

....

f) Which reward has an RRP of £35?

....

Notes

Spotting Similarities

You'll be asked to compare texts in your assessment — this includes finding similarities between them.

Similarities Are Alike or the Same

Texts Can Share Similar Ideas

Texts might share the same **themes**, **information** or **conclusions**.
Some texts share the exact same idea and some texts only share parts of an idea.

Texts can also have similar audiences and formats.

Use the Main Points to Find Similarities

1) Find each text's **main** points. → Text A describes train services positively. Text B describes bus services positively.

2) See whether these points **match**. → E.g. Both texts are in favour of public transport.

3) If they do — you've found a similarity. → E.g. "Text A and Text B agree that public transport is useful."

Now Try This

1) Read the following sentences.

   a) **Identify** the **two** sentences that share a similar opinion. Tick **two** boxes.

   "Video games are becoming far too expensive." ☐

   "Constant exposure to screens can damage your eyes." ☐

   "There's no real problem with video games." ☐

   "Staring at a computer for too long can give you a headache." ☐

   "Playing video games can teach you useful skills." ☐

   b) Give the opinion that the sentences share.

   ....

Section Two – Finding Information in Texts

Spotting Similarities

2) Read the texts below.

The Hills of Aiven
The Hills of Aiven are known for their amazing aspen trees. Unfortunately, 25% of the trees have been damaged by recent wildfires in the area. Experts suggest recovery will take up to 50 years. Locals have started a planting initiative which will speed up the process.

Natural Beauty Spots — Firsk Reserve
The nature reserve at Firsk still feels like the wilderness, despite a quarter of its forest being hit by wildfires last year.
Efforts to help the reserve heal have begun, but it seems unlikely that the forest will return to normal for decades, if not longer.

Give two pieces of information present in **both** of the texts.

1: ....

2: ....

3) Read the following texts.

Text A:

Volunteers Wanted!
Volunteering at the library gives you a chance to get involved with your local community. There are many benefits to working here:

- Make new friends!
- Great work experience.
- Free tea, coffee and biscuits.
- Access to learning resources.

Text B:

Should you join a book club?
Book clubs are a popular way to make friends in your neighbourhood. Not only that, but they are a great way to learn new things!
Studies suggest that discussing books in a group helps our understanding of them.
Why not join a book club today? <u>Click here</u> to find one near you!

For each statement below, circle to say whether it is **true** or **false**.

Both texts suggest people should read more books.	True / False
Both texts suggest a way to make new friends.	True / False
Both texts offer work experience.	True / False
Both texts offer an opportunity for learning.	True / False
Both texts suggest local communities are important.	True / False

Notes

Spotting Differences

Finding differences between texts is an important skill — and it's a skill you need to develop.

Differences Provide a Contrast

Texts Can Disagree with Each Other

Different authors may have different opinions on the same topic.
Authors might disagree on everything, or just one or two specific points.

Learn the Types of Differences Between Texts

Texts can differ in several ways, for example:

- **Amount of detail** ➡ Are full explanations or brief summaries given?

- **Type of information** ➡ Are more facts or opinions used?

- **Agreement** ➡ Are different conclusions reached in each text?

Now Try This

1) Read the following sentences. **Identify** the sentence that has a different opinion from the others. Tick **one** box.

   "Music streaming services are incredibly convenient." ☐

   "I enjoy not having to rely on physical copies of music." ☐

   "It's so easy to play music from your phone." ☐

   "CDs and records are still enjoyed by music fans." ☐

2) Read the following text.

   > *We asked fashion experts Iben Selmer and Louis Rourke about upcoming trends:*
   > IS: I think designers of today have to recognise that the bigger fashion houses aren't going to keep up with trends. They have to set trends — not blindly follow them.
   > LR: It's about understanding the people buying the clothes. I'd love to see more from designers who aren't afraid to reflect modern tastes and respond to today's trends.

   What is **one** difference of opinion between Iben and Louis?

   ....

Spotting Differences

3) Read the following texts.

Text A:

Smell the coffee and wake up!
Coffee is a great way to increase your energy whenever you're feeling tired. Coffee always improves your mood and gives you that pep in your step you need to get you through a long day. Spreading cups of coffee out over your day can keep you focused and awake. To me, drinking coffee is the secret to happiness.

Text B:

Experts recommend avoiding coffee in the eight hours before going to bed:
- Caffeine's awakening effect peaks after 30-60 minutes, but it can last much longer.
- This reduces the quality of your sleep.

Any boost in energy after drinking a coffee can therefore be outweighed by extra tiredness in the long run due to poor sleep. This can cause low moods and irritation.

a) Read the following opinions.
   Draw a line from each opinion to show if it is different or shared by the two texts.

   Drinking coffee has several benefits.

   Drinking coffee can keep you awake.

   Shared opinion

   Drinking coffee affects your mood.

   Different opinion

   Drinking coffee gives you more energy.

   You should only drink coffee early in the day.

b) Which text suggests that drinking coffee makes people feel happier?
   Give one example from the text to support your answer.

   Text: ....   Example: ....

c) Name one organisational feature that is unique to each text.

   A: ....   B: ....

Notes

Section Three — Comparisons

Comparing Information and Ideas

Making comparisons is like weighing up pros and cons — it can help you to make a decision.

Comparisons Help You to Evaluate Texts

Comparing involves spotting similarities and differences, then using them to reach a conclusion. You can include your own opinions on the texts when making a comparison.

Look for Comparable Features

You'll need to compare more than one text as part of your reading exam.

1) **Key Points**:

   — Both authors **like** taking the bus...

   I enjoy catching the bus, but it's expensive. | The bus is fun and the fares are reasonable.

   ...but they **disagree** on the **cost** of bus fares.

2) **Use of Facts**:

   2 in 5 people prefer trains to buses. | One of these texts uses facts. The other presents opinions. | I think that's a lie.

3) **Style and Tone**:

   — Both authors use an **advisory** style...

   You should catch the 9 am train. | You'd better hop on the 10 am bus.

   ...but one is **formal**, and the other is **informal**.

Use Comparing Words to Highlight Differences

You can draw attention to differences by using **language** that makes a comparison.
E.g. *More / Less / In contrast / On the other hand / Similarly* etc.

Now Try This

1) Read the following texts.

   Are you sitting comfortably?
   A survey of the office shows 67% of our employees experience mild back pain. This can be caused by slouching at your desk, lifting heavy objects or even wearing ill-fitting footwear.

   Dr. Yeung, spine injury specialist.
   If you have damaged your spine, or want advice on how to avoid back injuries, talk to Dr. Yeung. Learn how to improve your posture and strengthen your back muscles.

   Which of the following is mentioned by **both** texts? **Tick one** box.

   Uncomfortable shoes ☐   Bad posture ☐   Avoiding back pain ☐

Comparing Information and Ideas

2) Read the following texts.

Text A:

Reference number: 6733

I would like to submit a report about the bus service between Ryd and Hatlew.
The bus only runs once a day — this is nowhere near enough. The service itself is already badly run. Last time I used the service, the bus was over half an hour late and missed three stops.

Text B:

⚠ **Notice to Passengers** ⚠

Next week, we are limiting the Ryd-Hatlew bus service. The bus will now run just once a day. This is due to a shortage of drivers. Passengers are advised to organise alternative travel arrangements. The bus will be extremely full and we cannot guarantee seats.

a) Which text has a more negative tone? Tick **one** box.

Text A ☐   Text B ☐

b) Give **one** quotation to support your answer to part (a).

....

c) Write down **one** piece of information from Text B that Text A **does not** mention.

....

d) Write down **one** piece of information that **both** texts mention.

....

e) For each statement below, circle to say whether it is **true** or **false**.

Both texts provide advice.	**True / False**
Both texts mention an alternative travel route.	**True / False**
Both texts describe a problem.	**True / False**
Both texts have an informal style.	**True / False**
Both texts provide factual information.	**True / False**

Notes

Comparing Opinions

Authors often have different opinions, and you need to be able to compare these to each other.

Some Opinions Are More Obvious Than Others

Remember That Opinions Are Personal

- Opinions are based on **feelings**.
- They are not factual and **cannot be proven**.

See pages 8-9 for more information about opinions.

Opinions Aren't Always Clear

You might have to work out an author's opinion before you can compare it.

1) **Think about the tone of the text.**
   E.g. A text with an upbeat tone is more likely to be expressing a positive opinion.
2) **Compare the language of the opinions.**
   E.g. An author who uses lots of emotive language is usually expressing a strong opinion.
   An author who uses lots of technical language is usually well-informed on the subject.

The Same Topic Can Produce Different Opinions

Authors can react differently to the same events or news.

Triumphant Return of Beavers to Boardtown	Beavers Plague Boardtown Residents
Uses **positive** language and suggests the event is beneficial.	Uses **negative** language and suggests the event is a problem.

Now Try This

1) Read the following texts.

   Text A:
   > This was a fairly good recipe, and I'm pleased with how the cake turned out. I'm not sure I melted the chocolate properly, but it tasted alright in the end.

   Text B:
   > This cake recipe calls for some technical precision. You have to temper the chocolate before putting it on top of the cake, which gives it a beautiful finish.

   In which text does the author seem more knowledgeable about baking?
   Give **one** reason to support your answer.

   Text: .... Reason: ....

Comparing Opinions

2) Read the following texts.

Text A:

> I think office dress codes are outdated. We work better when we're relaxed. Who feels relaxed when they are constantly made to wear clothes they don't feel comfortable in? Not me!

Text B:

> The problem with workplace dress codes is that the clothes can be expensive. Not everyone can afford to go out and buy new shirts or smart shoes. Workplaces with a dress code should cover the cost of employees' clothes.

Text C:

> Some people find dress codes too strict. However, dress codes help everyone in a workplace to feel like part of the team, and avoid any issues with inappropriate clothing. They maintain a professional tone in the work environment by ensuring that everyone looks respectable. Also, they make employees easily recognisable to customers.

a) Which text is the most **positive** about workplace dress codes? **Tick one** box.

Text A ☐   Text B ☐   Text C ☐

b) Give **one** reason for your answer to part (a).

....

c) Which of the following best describes Text B's opinion? **Tick one** box.

Workplaces struggle to find a uniform that suits everyone. ☐

The cost of new clothes can be a problem for employees. ☐

Workplaces shouldn't have a dress code at all. ☐

d) Which text suggests that dress codes can benefit customers?
Give **one** example from the text to support your answer.

Text: .....   Reason: ....

Notes

How Information is Conveyed

Information can be put across to the reader in different ways and using a variety of techniques.

Information Can be Conveyed Using Many Techniques

The way information is conveyed means 'how information is passed on to the reader'.

The Layout Guides You to Useful Information

See pages 22-25 for more on organisational features.

- Headings, subheadings and paragraphs are used to **organise** information.
- Different **types** of text will organise information in different ways:

  Instructive and **advisory** texts split information into **clear steps**.

  Discussive and **explanatory** texts use longer, more **detailed paragraphs**.

  Persuasive texts often put the most **important information** at the **start** and **end**.

Word Choices Can Influence the Reader

- Words that suggest **possibility** are used to present **ideas** and make the reader think.
  E.g. *Could, might, this suggests...*
- Data and words that show **certainty** are used to present **facts** and to convince the reader.
  E.g. *Studies show, research proves, 80% of...*

Language Techniques Can Make Texts Persuasive

- Persuasive texts often **directly address** the reader.
- They may also use catchy phrases and imaginative language to make them more **memorable**.

Now Try This

1) Read the following text.

   Hallengate Fruit Market — Farm Fresh Fruit!

   Hallengate Fruit Market runs every Wednesday morning in Hallengate car park. You can find it opposite the Newburn bus stop. All fruit is locally grown and the sellers take pride in the quality of their produce. They start setting up their stalls at 9 am

   - Apples — £1.10 / kg
   - Oranges — £1.30 / kg
   - Pears — £1.65 / kg
   - Bananas — £1 / kg

   Which of the following techniques does the text use to convey information?
   Circle three techniques.

   Quotations   Bullet points   Emotive language

   Direct address   A slogan

How Information is Conveyed

2) Read the following texts.

   Text A:

   > DRESS REHEARSAL!
   > The first rehearsal takes place at 4 pm tomorrow. We ask all performers to be punctual, prepared and in their costumes. The exact timings for each scene will be available on the group noticeboard later this afternoon.

   Text B:

   > Drama coursework assignment
   > Students are expected to have read both of the required plays on the course, and to understand their plots and themes. Students' essays should demonstrate a precise knowledge of theatre and stage design.

   Which of the following statements about the language used in the texts is correct?

   Both texts use the rule of three to be memorable. ☐

   Both texts use formal language to seem serious. ☐

   Both texts use alliteration to be catchy. ☐

   Both texts use imaginative language to show certainty. ☐

3) Read the following texts.

   Text A:

   > According to a recent study, the use of online learning in schools has increased by 85%. It provides students with an interactive way to learn, and gives them access to thousands of resources.

   Text B:

   > This school is becoming too dependent upon online learning. I understand that it gives our students access to lots of new resources, but we now use online resources for most lessons — if we have a power cut, we are in trouble.

   Give **one** quotation from each text to show that online learning is becoming more popular in schools.

   Text A: ....

   Text B: ....

Notes

Section Four – Reference Materials

Using Reference Materials

Reference materials like dictionaries and thesauruses help you to find the words you need.

You Can Look Up Tricky Words

Dictionaries Tell You the Meaning of a Word

- A dictionary tells you what a word **means** and how to **spell** it.

    You can use a dictionary in the reading exam.

    The word → **Palm** (pa:m) *n* 1 inner surface of the hand 2 a type of tree
    - How the word is said: (pa:m)
    - The type of word it is, e.g. noun, verb, adjective, etc.
    - One meaning of the word: inner surface of the hand
    - Another meaning of the word: a type of tree

- There are also **online** dictionaries — but you **can't** use these in your exam.

Dictionaries List Words in Alphabetical Order

- This means all words beginning with the same letter are grouped together.
- Words are then arranged into alphabetical order by their remaining letters.
  E.g. 'b**a**t' appears before 'b**e**e' in the dictionary.

Don't Rely on a Dictionary in the Exam

- Looking up the meanings of words can take time and slow you down.
- Sometimes you'll be able to work out the meaning of a word from the sentence it's in.

Now Try This

1) Use a dictionary to find a definition for each of the following words.

   Concur: ....

   Candid: ....

   Imminent: ....

   Pensive: ....

Using Reference Materials

2) Read the following sentences and write down what you think the words in **bold** mean.

   a) The angry customer in the shop was so rude, his manners were **abysmal**.

   ....

   b) July was so hot: there was a **minuscule** amount of rain.

   ....

   c) Now use a **dictionary** to look up the definitions of both words.

   abysmal: ....   minuscule: ....

3) Read the following text.

   > Learning a second language has ① **numerous** social and professional benefits. People who speak multiple languages often find that their problem-solving skills and memory are ② **enhanced** by their language abilities.
   > Businesses may prefer employees who can speak multiple languages because they can ③ **liaise** with international clients and companies. Speaking more than one language also ④ **establishes** understanding between cultures and grows relationships across diverse groups of people. Despite these ⑤ **obvious** advantages, many people hesitate to learn a second language because of the time and effort ⑥ **required**. However, experts suggest that with consistent practice, anyone can achieve fluency in a second language.

   Use a **dictionary** to look up definitions for the words numbered 1-6.

   1: ....   2: ....   3: ....

   4: ....   5: ....   6: ....

Notes

Using Reference Materials

You can read more effectively and find key information more quickly by using reference materials.

Texts Can Contain Reference Materials

Referencing Can Guide You Through a Text

Texts have their own ways of directing readers to **useful** content. Knowing how to use these can help you find information **faster**.

Indexes and glossaries are usually listed in alphabetical order.

Reference Feature	Where to Find Them	Purpose
Table of Contents	At the **start** of a text.	To show what each page or section is **about**.
Index	At the **end** of a text.	To help readers to find **specific** topics or terms.
Glossary	At the **end** of a text.	To provide **definitions** of key terms.
Appendix	At the **end** of a text.	To provide **extra** information.
Footnote	At the **bottom** of a page.	To provide **definitions** or **extra** information without interrupting the main text.

Now Try This

1) Read the following text.

MENU CONTENTS

Appetisers and Nibbles 1
Soups and Salads 2
Sides & Sharing Plates 3
Main Dishes 5
Wines 8
Cocktails 10
Hot drinks 11
Soft drinks 12

a) On which page would you find the following items?

Coffee: ....   Salads: ....

b) What would you find on the following pages?

Page 8: ....   Page 4: ....

Section Four – Reference Materials

Using Reference Materials

2) **Draw a line** to match each scenario below to the reference material you would use.

Scenario	Reference
You read a book about gardening and want to find the section about fertiliser.	Table of contents
You want more detailed information about the subject of an academic text.	Index
A book has 150 pages on frogs, but you only want to learn about bullfrogs.	Glossary
You find a word that you don't understand in a book.	Appendix

3) Read the following text.

> This week, our researchers in the environmental department unveiled their plans for a pesticide* that does not affect bees.
> Modern pesticides can cause lasting neurological** damage to bees, often resulting in paralysis*** and, eventually, death.
>
> * pesticide — a chemical used on crops to kill insects.
> ** neurological — involving the nerves.
> *** paralysis — inability to move.   —A
>
> Aske Research Institute
> *est. 1902*

a) What reference feature is labelled A? Underline one option.

Index / **Footnote** / **Appendix**

b) Give one reason for your answer to part (a).

....

c) Suggest **two** key terms from the text that could be included in an **index**.

Term 1: ....   Term 2: ....

Notes

Identifying Information

Read the following text and answer the questions on the next page.

The FUTURE of fashion

It's time for some forward thinking. Mohan Persaud gives us the facts.

Fast fashion frenzy!

The fashion industry produces over 90 million tonnes of fabric waste a year, and less than 1% of this is recycled.

Much of this is due to fast fashion, which produces cheap and low-quality clothes at an unsustainable rate.

A change in season

Fashion is an industry built around trends, demanding new ideas for each season. Recently, talk in the industry has revolved around sustainable clothing. This involves making sure that the process of making, selling and disposing of clothes causes as little environmental harm as possible.

Material worth

Sustainable fashion can be carried out in a range of ways, by both fashion brands and consumers. On the production side, there is the option to start using fabrics with less environmental impact. For example, organic cotton can be produced using less water and fewer chemicals than regular cotton.

Some brands are also experimenting with eco-friendly materials. Vegan leather can be made of anything from cactus leaves to corn to recycled plastic.

Production must make progress

Another more sustainable option is to use renewable energies in production, such as wind, solar and hydropower. An additional issue to be aware of is how materials are often transported huge distances to produce clothes. Investing in local materials is far better for the environment.

Make good choices

When it comes to the consumer side of things, it's all about making considered decisions. Part of this is knowing the difference between *wanting* and *needing* new items of clothing. The rising "slow fashion" movement prioritises clothing quality over quantity, encouraging consumers to buy fewer but longer-lasting clothes. This creates less waste, as well-made clothes don't wear out as quickly, and people are able to keep them for longer.

Anyone for seconds?

Lately, the popularity of secondhand clothing has rocketed. Consumers are realising that they can find high-quality, stylish pieces without having to buy them brand new. This reduces demand for new clothes and minimises fabric waste — a win-win situation.

Just last month, the Milanese fashion house of Carago Fazio dedicated the majority of their Spring collection to the reuse of older designs. The show was a tremendous success, with many saying that it had inspired them to go back through their wardrobes and find a second life for clothes they might otherwise have thrown away, or never worn again.

Whilst the industry still faces challenges, the interest in eco-friendly clothing is a step in the right direction. By embracing sustainable practices, the fashion industry can keep us looking stylish forever.

Identifying Information

1) What is the main point of this text? Tick **one** box.

    A To explain the history of fashion trends. ☐

    B To explain changes in the fashion industry. ☐

    C To explain the possible benefits of fast fashion. ☐

2) Which of the following is an example of sustainable fashion mentioned in the text? Tick **one** box.

    A Using tradition fabrics such as silk and wool. ☐

    B Producing more clothing to meet higher demand. ☐

    C Using eco-friendly materials such as organic cotton. ☐

3) Which of the following does the text advise fashion brands to do? Tick **one** box.

    A Avoid using renewable energy sources like wind and solar. ☐

    B Only make clothes that are 100% recyclable. ☐

    C Use local materials to produce their clothes. ☐

4) What does the term "slow fashion" refer to in the text? Tick **one** box.

    A The trend of buying cheap or badly made clothes. ☐

    B A movement that focuses on buying high-quality clothes. ☐

    C Fashionable clothing that is only made of recycled materials. ☐

5) According to the text, why are secondhand clothes becoming more popular? Tick **one** box.

    A They are a sustainable alternative to brand-new clothes. ☐

    B They require less time to produce. ☐

    C They last longer than brand-new clothes. ☐

6) Which of the following best describes the text's tone? Tick **one** box.

    A Informative and persuasive. ☐

    B Objective and neutral. ☐

    C Humorous and casual. ☐

Notes

Facts, Opinions & Bias

Read the following text and answer the questions on the next page.

From: J.Howard@azmail.co.uk
Subject: Concern about local recycling initiatives

 RecyclingBinMistakes... 203 Kbs

 NewRecyclingInitiative... 437 Kbs

Received at 7:57 am November 25th 2024.

Dear Councillor Bradshaw,

I am writing to express my concerns about the new recycling programme being introduced in our district. I understand that the aim of the programme is to reduce waste and improve recycling rates, but I believe this programme has several major flaws.

Firstly, the programme's introduction has been rushed. The new green bins arrived one day late and many residents, including myself, were not properly informed about how to correctly separate their waste. This lack of clear communication has caused a great deal of confusion. I have already seen numerous mistakes in the bins where recyclables have been mixed with non-recyclables — please see the photo I have attached above.

Secondly, the new programme lacks clarity regarding its environmental impact. In the original proposal, which I have attached above as a reminder, the council claimed that the programme would reduce landfill waste by 40%. However, there is no data provided to back up this claim. Without clear evidence, I find it hard to believe this number.

Furthermore, several local businesses have already complained that the new recycling guidance will force them to make expensive changes to how they process waste. This could make it harder for them to stay open — and small independent businesses are already struggling. I doubt the council has even considered this.

It seems to me that the council has prioritised looking good over doing something that is actually beneficial to local residents. I worry that the push for this programme is more to appear environmentally conscious than to benefit the environment. Councillor Bradshaw, I urge you to reconsider this programme.

I ask that you improve communication with residents, make supporting data more easily available to the public and consider how local businesses are being affected by the programme.

Thank you for your attention to these matters. I look forward to receiving your response.

Kind regards,

Jane Howard.

Facts, Opinions & Bias

1) Which of the following quotations from the text contains a fact? Tick **one** box.

   A "The new green bins arrived one day late" ☐

   B "Without clear evidence, I find it hard to believe this number" ☐

   C "It seems to me that the council has prioritised looking good" ☐

2) Which of the following quotations from the text expresses an opinion? Tick **one** box.

   A "the aim of the programme is to reduce waste" ☐

   B "I believe this programme has several major flaws" ☐

   C "several local businesses have already complained" ☐

3) Which of the following quotations from the text is an example of bias? Tick **one** box.

   A "the programme's introduction has been rushed" ☐

   B "please see the photo I have attached above" ☐

   C "I look forward to receiving your response" ☐

4) Which of the following facts is **not** included in the text? Tick **one** box.

   A The percentage that the council expects to reduce landfill by. ☐

   B How many new recycling bins the author received. ☐

   C What colour the bins for the new recycling programme are. ☐

5) Which of these sentences best represents the author's opinion? Tick **one** box.

   A There are not enough recycling bins available. ☐

   B Small businesses shouldn't need to recycle. ☐

   C The new recycling programme has not been thought through. ☐

6) Which of the following would make the text less biased? Tick **one** box.

   A Using more emotive language to express disappointment. ☐

   B Including information on the programme's achievements. ☐

   C Comparing this programme to a more effective one. ☐

Notes

Organisational Features

Read the following text and answer the questions on the next page.

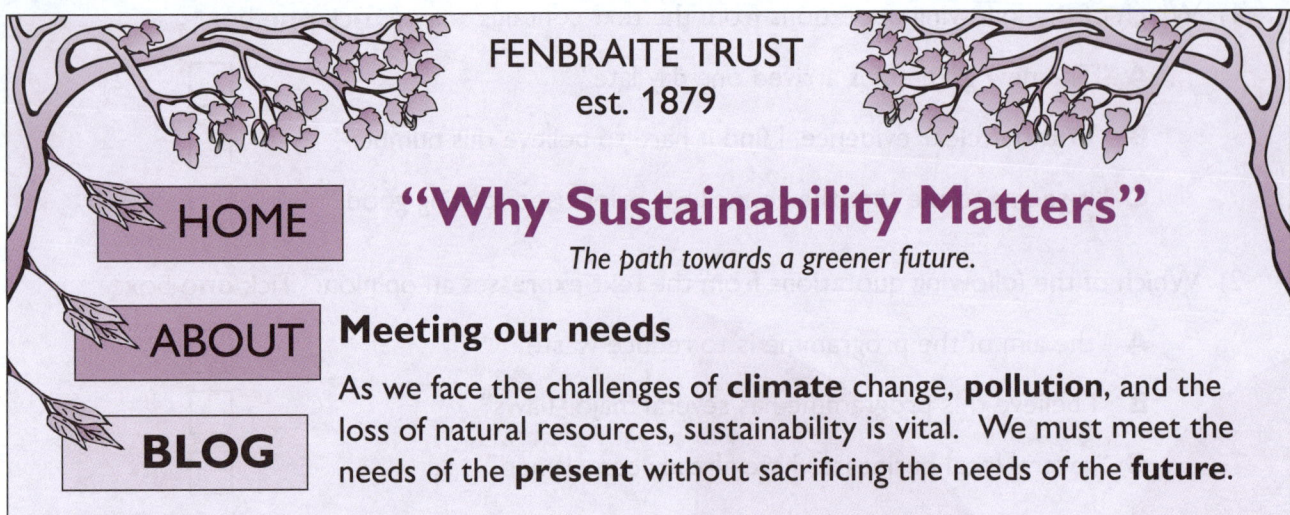

FENBRAITE TRUST
est. 1879

HOME

"Why Sustainability Matters"
The path towards a greener future.

ABOUT

Meeting our needs

As we face the challenges of **climate** change, **pollution**, and the loss of natural resources, sustainability is vital. We must meet the needs of the **present** without sacrificing the needs of the **future**.

BLOG

Protecting our planet

Environmental sustainability means preserving our **natural** resources. These resources include the water we drink, the air we breathe, the soil beneath our feet and even the animals we share the planet with. In order to preserve these things, we need to focus on reducing **waste**, saving **water**, and protecting our wildlife **habitats**. *To read about ongoing environmental projects at Fenbraite, click the link buttons below:*

 Habitat Havens

 Recycle Right

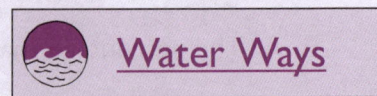 Water Ways

Growth without greed

Economic sustainability involves creating a **balance** within our society that allows the economy to grow without harming the environment. This can be achieved by reducing **energy** consumption and by using **renewable** energy sources. Click the **"HOME"** button above to see advice on reducing energy costs.

All in it together

A socially sustainable community is one where resources are shared out equally. We must ensure that all communities have **access** to essential services and resources. Next month, Fenbraite is hosting a series of talks about social sustainability. These will be given by visiting lecturer Janhavi Gupta. *See below for details.*

Lecture Title	Date and Time
"Raising Our Voices: Eco-Poetry"	12th January, 7:30 pm
"How Can We Teach Our Children?"	14th January, 7:30 pm
"Community and Caring"	15th January, 11 am

Organisational Features

1) How is the information in the webpage organised? Tick **one** box.

   A Long paragraphs with footnotes. ☐

   B Short, bullet-pointed lists. ☐

   C Clearly titled sections. ☐

2) Which of the following is used to guide readers to information about environmental projects? Tick **one** box.

   A A table of information. ☐

   B A series of links. ☐

   C A subheading. ☐

3) Which reason best describes why the headline is in coloured text? Tick **one** box.

   A To match the tone of the webpage. ☐

   B To make the author's argument stronger. ☐

   C To make it stand out from the rest of the text. ☐

4) What is the subheading for the section about economic sustainability? Tick **one** box.

   A Protecting our planet ☐

   B Growth without greed ☐

   C All in it together ☐

5) What feature informs readers about the series of talks Fenbraite is hosting? Tick **one** box.

   A A table of information. ☐

   B A link within the text. ☐

   C A relevant graphic. ☐

6) What feature is used to make keywords stand out in each paragraph? Tick **one** box.

   A Italics ☐

   B Different fonts ☐

   C Bolding ☐

Notes

Language Features

Read the following text and answer the questions on the next page.

>   Mark Copps
>   Head of Research
>   Ecological Research Dept.
>   Derford, Wornley
>   *11th July*
>
> Complaints Department
> Delmnett & Sons
> Cormlett Industrial Park
> Cormlett, EG89 3EX
>
> Dear Sir / Madam,
>
> I am writing to you about your carbon emissions. I believe they are a dark shadow over our town's reputation. As a climate researcher, I know firsthand how dangerous excessive carbon emissions can be, and I am deeply anxious about the lack of urgency with which your company has addressed its environmental impact. Your carbon emissions have a significant negative effect and it's high time you took decisive action to limit them. Is anything more important?
>
> I understand that reducing emissions can be difficult, but there are many practical and effective measures your company could put in place. For example — using renewable energy, making your processes more energy-efficient, and investing in carbon offset programmes. Your company can choose change — you can help us to improve the carbon footprint of our local area and guarantee a greener future for all of us.
>
> These changes will require honesty, commitment and cooperation. Moreover, they may also increase your costs. If there is anything that we at the Ecological Research Department can do to help, please let me know. We would be more than happy to provide guidance and help to raise funds. After all, this planet is home to us all.
>
> Please send a response outlining the steps that you are willing to take to address this important issue immediately. I look forward to hearing about any measures you plan to introduce in the future.
>
> Regards,
>
> Mark Copps

Language Features

1) What language technique is used in the phrase "they are a dark shadow"? Tick **one** box.

   A A direct question ☐

   B A simile ☐

   C A metaphor ☐

2) Which of the following is an example of alliteration? Tick **one** box.

   A "it's high time you took decisive action" ☐

   B "this planet is home to us all" ☐

   C "address this important issue immediately" ☐

3) Why is emotive language used in the phrase "I am deeply anxious"? Tick **one** box.

   A To make the sentence more informal. ☐

   B It makes the phrase more memorable. ☐

   C To appeal to the reader's feelings. ☐

4) What persuasive technique is used in the phrase "honesty, commitment and cooperation"? Tick **one** box.

   A The rule of three ☐

   B A slogan ☐

   C A rhetorical question ☐

5) What style of writing is used in the phrase "send a response"? Tick **one** box.

   A Explanatory ☐

   B Instructive ☐

   C Descriptive ☐

6) Why is direct address used in the phrase "Your company can choose change"? Tick **one** box.

   A To make the text more persuasive. ☐

   B To make the text more formal. ☐

   C To make the text more entertaining. ☐

Notes

Making Comparisons

Read the following text and answer the questions on the next page.

Ecolo Echo — FORUM

POST 1 — GreenWarrior86 — *1 day ago*

Recycling is one of the easiest and most effective ways we can reduce waste and help save the planet. Every year, tonnes of paper, plastic and metal are thrown away, but they could be reused if we simply took the time to separate them. It's so straightforward to do, and there are plenty of resources available online if you need more advice. Besides, recycling doesn't just reduce pollution — it also saves energy and natural resources. We all need to make a small effort in our daily lives to recycle more, whether that's sorting our waste at home or encouraging businesses to adopt sustainable practices. It's a simple step towards a better future and something that everyone can get involved in alongside other actions such as volunteering with community clean-up projects.

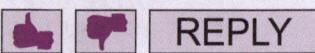

POST 2 — EcoExpert99 — *3 hours ago*

I recognise that recycling is important, but it's not the only solution to our waste problem. The obvious issue here is that we're creating *too much waste* in the first place. If we can reduce our reliance upon single-use plastics — especially shopping bags and water bottles — and try to choose reusable items instead, we won't have as much waste to recycle in the first place. Recycling needs to be part of a larger movement towards sustainability, but *we can't depend upon recycling* as our only option. The real change will come when we rethink our habits and pay attention to the decisions that we make. The next time you go to recycle or even bin something, ask yourself if you could find another use for it. It's *reduce, reuse, recycle*, and we should keep that order in mind.

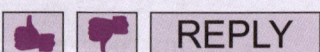

POST 3 — WasteNot1 — *6 minutes ago*

I get it, there are loads of good things about recycling. But what about the *challenges*? It's just silly to think it's totally straightforward. So many people don't know how to recycle *properly*, and some materials can't even be recycled in the first place. And what about contamination? When recyclable materials get mixed up with non-recyclables, like last night's dinner, the recyclable materials can't be processed correctly. It's tempting to ignore the problems and pretend it's a piece of cake. However, we've got to *educate ourselves and others* about good recycling practices. By coming together as a community to learn how recycling works, we can start to improve. Collaboration is a really awesome way to bring people together and show how small actions can add up to much bigger changes.

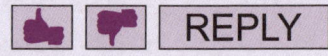

Making Comparisons

1) Which statement about Post 1 and Post 2 is true? Tick **one** box.

    A   Only Post 1 suggests people should recycle. ☐

    B   Only Post 2 suggests people should recycle. ☐

    C   Both posts suggest people should recycle. ☐

2) Which post has the most positive view of recycling? Tick **one** box.

    A   Post 1 ☐

    B   Post 2 ☐

    C   Post 3 ☐

3) How do Post 2 and Post 3 convey their ideas in a similar way? Tick **one** box.

    A   Both use metaphors to help readers visualise the topic. ☐

    B   Both use italics to make important points stand out. ☐

    C   Both use the rule of three to emphasise their points. ☐

4) Which of the following suggestions is made by all three posts? Tick **one** box.

    A   People should use more reusable shopping bags. ☐

    B   Recycling needs to be done alongside other changes. ☐

    C   Businesses should separate all their waste. ☐

5) Which of the following is a difference between Post 1 and Post 3? Tick **one** box.

    A   Post 3 has a more informal style than Post 1. ☐

    B   Post 1 has a more informal style than Post 3. ☐

    C   Both posts have an equally formal style. ☐

6) What do Post 1 and Post 3 recommend that Post 2 doesn't? Tick **one** box.

    A   Focusing on the protection of natural resources. ☐

    B   Using online resources to learn about recycling. ☐

    C   Working with others to improve recycling habits. ☐

Notes

Exam-style Practice

Functional Skills

English — Level 2 — Reading

Exam-style practice

Instructions to candidates:

- There are three texts. Read each text carefully before you start answering the questions.

  Text A — article   Text B — online newsletter   Text C — social media post

- Make sure you understand each question before you start answering it.

- You may use a dictionary to help you answer the questions.

- You don't need to write in full sentences — spelling, punctuation & grammar will not be marked.

Text A
An article about a new retail park.

New Retail Park to Open in City Centre

A new retail park is set to open in the heart of the city, bringing a range of benefits to the local community. The new development, which is opening at the end of next year, will have 30 shops, several restaurants, a supermarket and a cinema. It will create more than 500 new jobs for locals and I believe this will give the local economy a major boost.

Securing a sustainable vision

The development is part of an ambitious plan to revitalise the city centre, while championing sustainable building practices and eco-friendly designs. The retail park will be powered by renewable energy and feature green spaces for visitors to enjoy. One member of the public told us, "I love to see large-scale projects that also consider the environment."

Introduction of high-quality retail outlets

The park will provide much-needed retail space for popular brands, which have been looking for opportunities to expand in this region. As well as meeting the increasing demand for high quality retail outlets in the local area, the park is expected to attract a large number of shoppers from across the county. By bringing more people to the city centre, it also bolsters business for existing retailers in the area.

Residents' traffic concerns

Residents have welcomed the plans, especially the job opportunities they will bring. However, some have voiced concerns about the impact on traffic congestion. Developers say they are working closely with city planners to keep any potential disruption from the park's construction to a minimum.

Exam-style Practice

Text B

An online newsletter about a new retail park.

 **Linfort Community Newsletter**
City matters in the city that matters.

Boosting the local economy

The Linfort City Council have <u>unveiled plans</u> for a new retail park that promises to bring a wide variety of shops and vital services to our area. The council have emphasised that the project will promote local businesses and create hundreds of <u>job opportunities</u> for locals. The project is expected to generate significant economic growth — not just from the retail stores themselves, but also by increasing tourism and spending in the surrounding area.

Consulting local communities

Linfort residents are largely enthusiastic about the new opportunities that the retail park will bring. Many look forward to the improved shopping experience and the convenience it will offer. However, there are mixed opinions about the environmental impact of the development.

Addressing residents' concerns

While the new retail park will have energy-efficient buildings and green spaces, some residents are concerned that it will bring more traffic to the city. The council have assured the community that they are working on a <u>detailed traffic management plan</u> to address these concerns. There will be ample parking for visitors, which should prevent other parts of the city from becoming a swamp of traffic.

Revitalising the city

The new retail park is an essential addition to the city. Many residents believe it will modernise an otherwise neglected part of the city — the historic old town. However, some are concerned that this will increase rent in the area. Despite this, overall feeling in the community is positive, with most being excited about the park's benefits.

Visit the council's website to learn more.

Text C

A social media post about a new retail park.

Exciting news for our city! — by Frank's Florals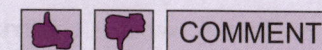

A new retail park is on its way, bringing shopping, dining and job opportunities to the heart of our community. With over 30 shops, restaurants and a supermarket, this development will create hundreds of jobs and attract more visitors to Linfort. It can only mean good things!

We're all thrilled about the economic boost this will bring, and we can't wait to see the immense positive impact it will have on our community — both Linfort residents and local businesses.

We're also happy to hear that sustainability is important to this project. It will feature green spaces and eco-friendly building practices. Isn't that great?

Let's keep supporting local industry and growing the Linfort economy!

Exam-style Practice

You will need to read Text A to answer questions 1 to 5.

1 Give **one** organisational feature from Text A. **Explain** the effect of this feature.

   Feature: ....

   Effect: ....
   [2]

2 You may use a dictionary to help you answer this question.
   Text A says that the retail park "bolsters business for existing retailers".
   What does the word "bolsters" mean?

   A Limits ☐   **C** Attracts ☐

   B Strengthens ☐   **D** Maintains ☐
   [1]

3 a) Identify **two** facts about the new retail park from Text A.

   1: ....

   2: ....
   [2]

   b) Identify **one** opinion from Text A.

   ....
   [1]

4 According to Text A, what is the **main concern** residents have about the new retail park?

   ....
   [1]

5 Use Text A to identify **two** ways that the new retail park will be environmentally friendly.

   1: ....

   2: ....
   [2]

Exam-style Practice

You will need to read Text B to answer questions 6 to 11.

6 In Text B, what is the subheading for the section about residents' concerns?

....
[1]

7 What best describes the style of Text B? Tick **one** box.

　A Humorous ☐　　**C** Advisory ☐

　B Instructive ☐　　**D** Informative ☐
[1]

8 Text B uses the phrase "a swamp of traffic".

　a) What language technique is used in this phrase? Tick **one** box.

　　A An idiom ☐　　**C** A metaphor ☐

　　B Alliteration ☐　　**D** A simile ☐
[1]

　b) Explain the effect this technique has on the reader.

....
[1]

9 According to Text B, decide whether the statements below are **true** or **false**.
Tick **one** box for each statement.

	True	False
The retail park will not provide enough parking space.	☐	☐
The retail park will benefit local businesses.	☐	☐
The retail park will be in a modern part of the city.	☐	☐

[3]

10 Give **one** feature from Text B that directs the reader to more information.

....
[1]

11 Give **two** quotations from Text B that suggest locals are looking forward to the retail park.

1: ....

2: ....
[2]

© CGP — not to be photocopied　　　　　　　　　　　　　　　　　　　　　　Exam-style Practice

Exam-style Practice

You will need to read Text B and Text C to answer questions 12 to 15.

12 Which **one** of the following statements from Text C is an example of bias? Tick **one** box.

　　A "A new retail park is on its way" ☐

　　B "sustainability is important to this project" ☐

　　C "It will feature green spaces and eco-friendly building practices" ☐

　　D "We're all thrilled about the economic boost this will bring" ☐

[1]

13 Give **one** example of persuasive language from Text C. Explain its effect on the reader.

Example: ....

Effect: ....

[2]

14 Text B and Text C give different information about the new retail park.
　　Compare how the information in these texts is different, using an example from each text.

....
....
....
....

[2]

15 Show a similarity or difference in the way that information about the retail park is conveyed in Text B and Text C. Use an example from each text.

....
....
....
....

[2]

About the Test

This page is full of information about the Reading Paper for Level 2 English — it'll prepare you in no time.

The Basics

The Reading component of Level 2 English is assessed with **one** test.

You might take this test on a **computer** (on screen) or on **paper**.

You will read a **range** of texts and **answer questions** about them. The texts will usually be about the **same topic**.

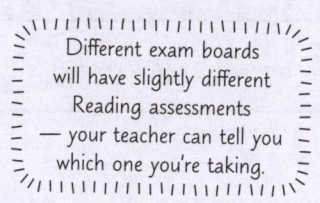
Different exam boards will have slightly different Reading assessments — your teacher can tell you which one you're taking.

- Some questions are **multiple choice** — you choose the correct answer.
- For some questions, you will have to **write** the answer down.
- Don't worry about your spelling, punctuation and grammar unless you're specifically asked about them — but try to make sure that your answers are **clearly written**.
- You are **not required** to write **full sentences**.
- You **can use** a **dictionary** in the test to look up any tricky words.

The amount of time you have depends on your exam board, but is usually **about 1 hour**.

Read the questions carefully — make sure you understand what you need to do before you answer.

How Will I be Marked?

This exam assesses your **reading** skills.
You will need to show your understanding of:

- different **types of texts** and their **purposes**.
- the various **features** of texts and how they add to their **meaning**.
- how texts can be **compared**.
- how texts **convey information**.
- writing **styles**, including the writer's **voice**, **formality** and **bias**.
- **reference materials** and other resources.

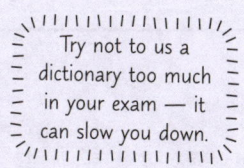
Try not to us a dictionary too much in your exam — it can slow you down.

Jot down information about the test you're going to be sitting here.

Notes

Individual Learning Plan

After each lesson or topic, use the table below to record your progress. Then you and your teacher can identify what you still don't feel confident with, why you found it difficult and what you can do to improve.

1. What I Can Do Now	2. What I Found Hard
Example: I can identify the purpose of a text	Identifying different styles of writing

Individual Learning Plan © CGP — not to be photocopied

Individual Learning Plan

If you want more space to write your plan, go to: cgpbooks.co.uk/fs-english or scan the QR code in the header to find a printable PDF of this table.

3. What I Need To Improve On	4. What I Will Do To Improve
Spotting idioms	Make a list of common idioms

Glossary

Advertisement (advert)	A text type that persuades the reader to do something, for example buy a product.
Alliteration	When words that are close together begin with the same sound.
Article	A text type usually found in newspapers or magazines.
Audience	The person or people who read a text.
Bias	When a text isn't balanced and only gives one point of view.
Bullet points	A way of breaking up information into separate points in a list.
Caption	Text that tells you more about a graphic.
Conversational tone	Chatty writing style normally found in informal texts.
Descriptive writing	Writing that tells the reader what something is like.
Direct address	Writing that uses 'you' to address the reader directly.
Emotive language	Language that appeals to the reader's feelings.
Explanatory writing	Writing that tells the reader about something.
Font	How letters look when they are typed, for example **bold** or *italics*.
Footnote	Extra information at the bottom of a page. Shown by small, raised numbers or symbols within a text.
Formal writing	A type of writing that sounds serious and professional.
Forum	A webpage where people discuss their opinions on a particular subject.
Graphic	A picture, diagram or chart.
Idiom	A commonly used saying which has a different set meaning to the literal meaning of the words.
Impersonal writing	Writing that doesn't tell you anything about the writer's personality or opinions.

Glossary

Informal writing	Writing that sounds chatty and friendly.
Instructive writing	Writing that tells the reader how to do something.
Layout	How a text is presented on the page using different organisational features.
Leaflet	A text type, usually given away for free, that gives information about something.
Letter	A text type written to a person, or group of people, which is sent in the post.
Metaphor	A way of describing something by saying it is something else.
Organisational features	Any feature of the text which affects how the text looks, e.g. colour or bullet points.
Personal writing	Text that is written from the author's point of view and uses emotional language and opinions. It sounds like it's talking to the reader.
Persuasive writing	Writing that tries to convince the reader to do or feel something.
Purpose	The reason a text is written, e.g. to persuade or to explain.
Report	A text type that gives information about something that has happened or may happen.
Rule of three	A list of three words or phrases used to create emphasis.
Simile	A way of describing something by comparing it to something else.
Slogan	A short, memorable phrase used in advertising.
Specialist words	Words specific to particular subjects or contexts.
Statistic	A numerical fact that is based on research or surveys.
Style	The way a text is written, e.g. a text may be formal, informal, advisory or humorous.
Tone	The way a text sounds to the reader, for example personal or impersonal.
Webpage	A document located on the internet.

CGP

www.cgpbooks.co.uk

Name ....

Functional Skills
English: Writing
Level 2

Course Booklet

Answers available online

CGP Books — The Choice of Champions!

They know it... you know it... everyone knows it!

cgpbooks.co.uk

Contents

✓ Use the tick boxes to check off the topics you've completed.

About This Booklet .... 1 ☐
Knowledge Organiser .... 2 ☐

Section One — Using Grammar

Writing Sentences .... 4 ☐
Use correct grammar — definite and indefinite articles.

Using Tenses .... 6 ☐
Use correct grammar — consistent use of a range of tenses.

Using Verbs Correctly .... 8 ☐
Use correct grammar — subject-verb agreement.

Modal Verbs .... 10 ☐
Use correct grammar and modality devices
(e.g. to express probability or desirability).

Grammar Practice .... 12 ☐
Use correct grammar (e.g. subject-verb agreement, consistent use of a range of tenses, definite and indefinite articles) and modality devices (e.g. to express probability or desirability).

Section Two — Using Correct Punctuation

Using Commas .... 14 ☐
Punctuate writing correctly.

Colons and Lists .... 16 ☐
Punctuate writing correctly.

Apostrophes .... 18 ☐
Punctuate writing correctly.

Inverted Commas and Quotation Marks .... 20 ☐
Punctuate writing correctly.

Punctuation Practice .... 22 ☐
Punctuate writing correctly using a wide range of punctuation markers (e.g. colons, commas, inverted commas, apostrophes and quotation marks.

Section Three — Using Correct Spelling

Spelling Rules and Plurals .... 24 ☐
Spell words used in work, study and daily life, including a range of specialist words.

Using Prefixes and Suffixes .... 26 ☐
Spell words used in work, study and daily life, including a range of specialist words.

Words That Are Often Misspelt .... 28 ☐
Spell words used in work, study and daily life, including a range of specialist words.

Section Four — Structure and Planning

Audience and Purpose .... 30 ☐
Write text of an appropriate level of detail and of appropriate length to meet the needs of purpose and audience.

Organising Your Writing .... 32 ☐
Organise writing for different purposes using appropriate format and structure.

Using Paragraphs .... 34 ☐
Construct complex sentences consistently and accurately, using paragraphs where appropriate.

Developing Sentences .... 36 ☐
Construct complex sentences consistently and accurately, using paragraphs where appropriate.

Writing that Flows .... 38 ☐
Convey clear meaning and establish cohesion using organisational markers effectively.

Exciting Openings .... 40 ☐
Communicate information, ideas and opinions clearly, coherently and effectively.

Powerful Conclusions .... 42 ☐
Communicate information, ideas and opinions clearly, coherently and effectively.

Planning Your Answer .... 44 ☐
Communicate information, ideas and opinions clearly, coherently and effectively.

Checking and Correcting .... 46 ☐
Communicate information, ideas and opinions clearly, coherently and effectively.

Section Five — Using the Right Language

Getting the Tone Right .... 48 ☐
Use different language and register suited to audience and purpose.

Writing Styles .... 50 ☐
Use different language and register suited to audience and purpose.

Formal and Informal Writing .... 52 ☐
Use different language and register suited to audience and purpose.

Giving Your Opinion..................................54 ☐
Communicate information, ideas and opinions
clearly, coherently and effectively.

Writing Persuasively...............................56 ☐
Use different language and register
suited to audience and purpose.

Section Six — Using the Right Format

Writing Emails...58 ☐
Organise writing for different purposes using
appropriate format and structure.

Writing Letters..60 ☐
Organise writing for different purposes using
appropriate format and structure.

Writing Articles and Blogs...................62 ☐
Organise writing for different purposes using
appropriate format and structure.

Writing Reports.......................................64 ☐
Organise writing for different purposes using
appropriate format and structure.

Writing Leaflets......................................66 ☐
Organise writing for different purposes using
appropriate format and structure.

Writing Adverts......................................68 ☐
Organise writing for different purposes using
appropriate format and structure.

Topic-based Questions

Audience, Purpose and Tone...............................70 ☐
Developing Sentences..72 ☐
Organisation and Structure.................................74 ☐
Communicating Clearly and Coherently...........76 ☐
Format and Layout...78 ☐
Language and Register..80 ☐

Exam-style Practice

Exam-style Practice...82 ☐

About the Test...87 ☐
Individual Learning Plan....................................88 ☐
Glossary..90 ☐

Unlock your Digital Extras

To get your free digital extras, go to **cgpbooks.co.uk/fs-english** or scan the QR code below.

This will take you to:
- An answer booklet
- More Individual Learning Plan pages
- A Knowledge Retriever

Published by CGP

Written by Helen Hindmarch

Reviewer: David Norden

Editors: Aimee Ashurst, Tom Carney, Polly Jackson,
Alex Thompson, Adam Worster

With thanks to Glenn Rogers and Hannah Roscoe for the proofreading.
With thanks to Beth Linnane for the copyright research.

Specification points in Contents contain public sector information
licensed under the Open Government Licence v3.0. https://www.
nationalarchives.gov.uk/doc/open-government-licence/version/3/

ISBN: 978 1 83774 211 0
Printed by Elanders Ltd, Newcastle upon Tyne.
Graphics from Corel®

Text, design, layout and original illustrations © Coordination
Group Publications Ltd (CGP) 2025 All rights reserved.

Photocopying this book is not permitted, even if you have a CLA licence.
Extra copies are available from CGP with next day delivery • 0800 1712 712 • www.cgpbooks.co.uk

About This Booklet

This course booklet supports your learning of the 'Writing' part of the Level 2 qualification.

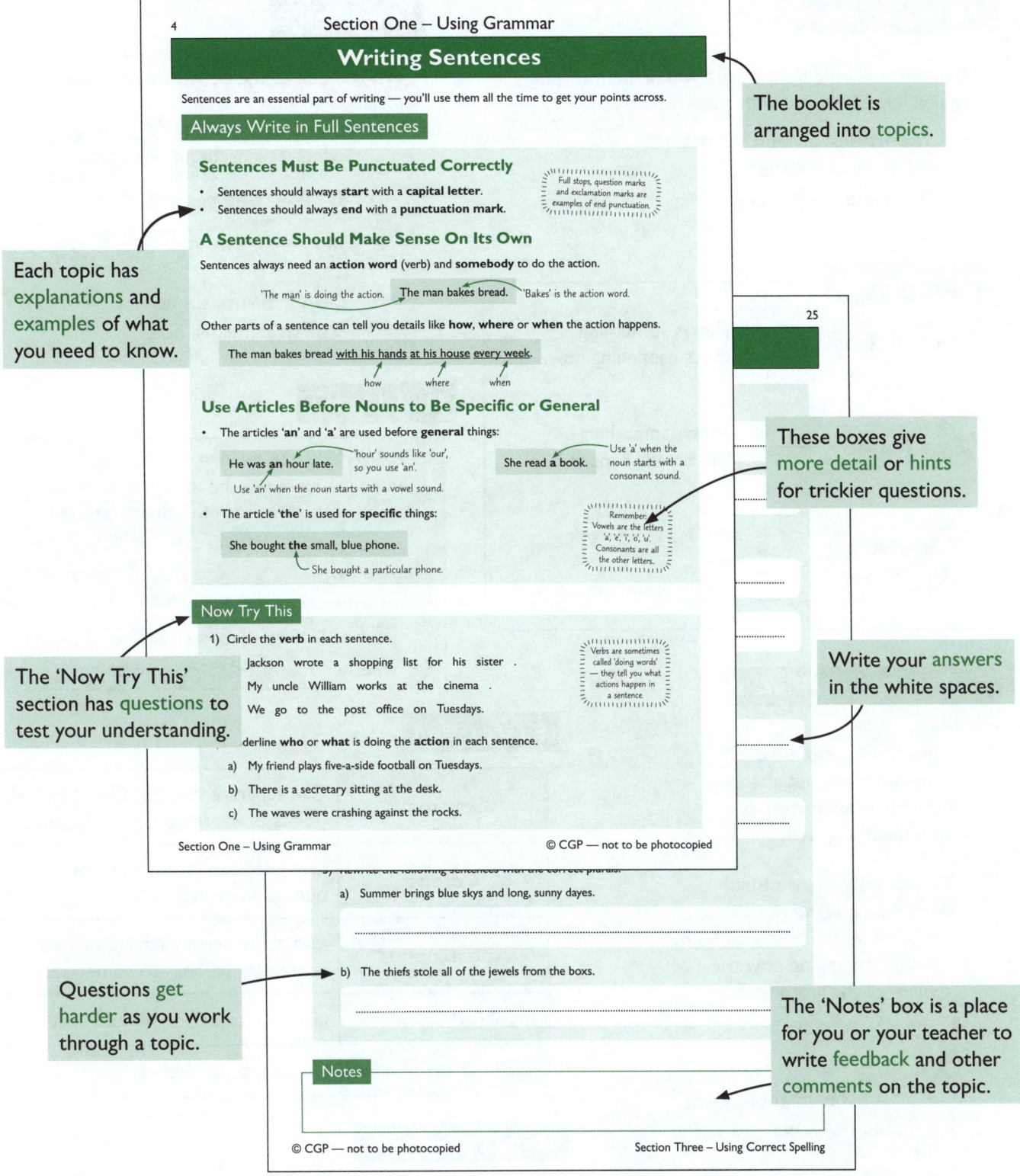

At the end of the booklet, you'll find:

- **Topic-Based Questions**: more practice — a variety of questions split into **topics**.
- **Exam-style Practice**: trickier tasks that will test you on **everything** from the booklet — you'll need to use **all of your writing skills** to answer these.
- **Individual Learning Plan**: to track your progress towards your **learning goals**.

Knowledge Organiser

There's plenty to learn when it comes to writing — here are some key bits to help you out.

Writing Sentences

Sentences should always **start** with a **capital letter** and **end** with a **punctuation mark**.
- The articles '**an**' and '**a**' are used before **general things**.
- The article '**the**' is used for **specific things**.

Using Verbs

Verbs need to **agree** with their subject:
- You often need to add '**s**' or '**es**' when talking about one person
- **is** ⟶ **one** person
- **are** ⟶ **two or more** people.

Don't means 'do not'.
Doesn't means 'does not'.

Using Tenses

Present Tense → Shows something that's happening now.

Past Tense → Shows something has already happened.

Talking About the Future → am / is / are + going
will + present tense verb

Modal Verbs

Modal verbs come **before** the main verb in a sentence. Here are the main modal verbs:

**Can Could May Might Shall Should
Will Would Must**

They show:
- how **likely** something is
- your **ability** to do something
- whether you **need** to do something

Modal verbs can be negative

Spelling Rules & Plurals

The 'i' before 'e' rule:
'i' before 'e' except after 'c', but only when it rhymes with 'bee'. E.g. bel**ie**ve.

You usually form plural words by adding an 's':
But some words follow different rules depending on how the spelling of the word ends.

- **Consonant then 'y'**
  Turn the 'y' into an 'i' and add 'es'.
- **Vowel then 'y'**
  Add an 's'.
- **'ch', 'x', 's', 'sh', 'z', 'o'**
  Add 'es'.
- **'f' or 'fe'**
  Change the 'f' to a 'v' and add 'es'.

Punctuation

Commas	Can separate items in a list, join two points or separate extra information.
Colons	Can introduce an explanation, quotation or list.
Apostrophes	Can show missing letters or that something belongs to someone.
Inverted Commas	Used for titles or to quote speech.
Quotation Marks	Used to quote speech.

Using Paragraphs

Paragraphs break your writing up into **smaller parts**.

To start a new paragraph: ⟶ Start a **new line** and leave a **space** at the beginning.

Use joining words in your writing to put your points in order, develop your writing and add examples.

Knowledge Organiser

Prefixes & Suffixes

Prefixes = letters added to the start of words.

dis + agree → **dis**agree

Suffixes = letters added to the end of words.

walk + ing → walk**ing**

Audience and Purpose

- Your audience is **who** you are writing for.
- Your purpose is **why** you are writing, e.g.

  to perform · to persuade

  to describe · to inform

  to entertain · to instruct

Giving Your Opinion

Make sure you can write how you **think** or **feel** about something. Support your opinions with **evidence**.

Write about other opinions to **balance** your argument.

Writing Formats

Different types of texts are used for different purposes:

- Emails
- Letters
- Articles
- Blogs
- Reports
- Leaflets
- Adverts
- Online Forums

Reports analyse an issue.

Leaflets and Adverts usually have to be persuasive.

Emails and letters follow a specific structure.

Articles are formal and informative whilst blogs and forums are usually more personal.

Writing Persuasively

Direct Address: Involves your audience in your writing.

Emotive Language: Language that appeals to the audience's feelings.

Alliteration: Repeated sounds at the start of words to make them more memorable.

The Rule of Three: Listing three related words emphasises a point.

Rhetorical Questions: Encourage people to agree with the writer.

Layout Features

Clearly **organise** your writing by using:

- Headings
- Subheadings
- Lists
- Tables

Style & Tone

Make sure you know when to use formal and informal writing.

Tone can be:
Personal or impersonal
Positive or negative

Style can be:
Explanatory Advisory
Humorous

These are just some common styles — there are many more.

Formal writing sounds serious and is usually used in professional situations.

Informal writing sounds chatty and is usually used with friends and family.

Planning Your Answer

- A plan should include your **key ideas**.
- Organise these ideas into a **logical order**.
- **Develop** your points when you write them by using joining words.
- **Check** and **correct** your writing.

Writing Sentences

Sentences are an essential part of writing — you'll use them all the time to get your points across.

Always Write in Full Sentences

Sentences Must Be Punctuated Correctly

- Sentences should always **start** with a **capital letter**.
- Sentences should always **end** with a **punctuation mark**.

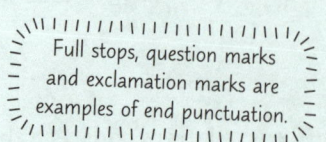
Full stops, question marks and exclamation marks are examples of end punctuation.

A Sentence Should Make Sense On Its Own

Sentences always need an **action word** (verb) and **somebody** to do the action.

'The man' is doing the action. → **The man** bakes bread. 'Bakes' is the action word.

Other parts of a sentence can tell you details like **how**, **where** or **when** the action happens.

The man bakes bread <u>with his hands</u> <u>at his house</u> <u>every week</u>.
                         how   where   when

Use Articles Before Nouns to Be Specific or General

- The articles '**an**' and '**a**' are used before **general** things:

  He was **an** hour late. — 'hour' sounds like 'our', so you use 'an'.

  She read **a** book. — Use 'a' when the noun starts with a consonant sound.

  Use 'an' when the noun starts with a vowel sound.

- The article '**the**' is used for **specific** things:

  She bought **the** small, blue phone. — She bought a particular phone.

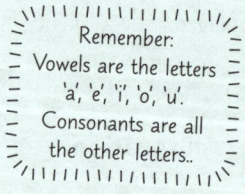
Remember: Vowels are the letters 'a', 'e', 'i', 'o', 'u'. Consonants are all the other letters.

Now Try This

1) Circle the **verb** in each sentence.

   a) Jackson wrote a shopping list for his sister .

   b) My uncle William works at the cinema .

   c) We go to the post office on Tuesdays.

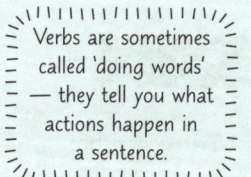
Verbs are sometimes called 'doing words' — they tell you what actions happen in a sentence.

2) Underline **who** or **what** is doing the **action** in each sentence.

   a) My friend plays five-a-side football on Tuesdays.

   b) There is a secretary sitting at the desk.

   c) The waves were crashing against the rocks.

Writing Sentences

3) For each sentence below, write **when** the action happens.

   a) I cook a pasta bake once a fortnight. ....

   b) Every other day, he goes to the corner shop. ....

4) Rewrite the sentence below by putting the articles in **bold** in the correct places.

   a) I went to **an** market to buy **a** apricot and **the** tomato .

   ....

5) Complete each sentence below by adding 'a' or 'an'.

   a) Well, I had .... unpleasant evening.

   Always use a capital 'I' to talk about yourself.

   b) Julia gave me .... one-pound coin to spend.

   c) They saw .... opening appear in the crowd.

6) Rewrite each sentence below with the correct **articles**.

   a) They came to understanding after debating for hour.

   ....

   b) It was gorgeous day because sun was shining.

   ....

   c) Do we need to buy couple of tickets?

   ....

Notes

Using Tenses

The verbs you use will change depending on when things happen — in the past, present or future.

There are Three Main Ways to Talk About Time

The Present Tense Shows Something is Happening Now

| I run | you run | we wash | they wash |

For 'I', 'you', 'we' or 'they', you don't need to change the verb.

| he run<u>s</u> | she run<u>s</u> | it wash<u>es</u> | Tom wash<u>es</u> |

For 'he', 'she', 'it' or someone's name, add 's' or 'es' to the verb.

The Past Tense Shows Something Has Already Happened

laugh ⟶ She laugh<u>ed</u>   they cook ⟶ they cook<u>ed</u>

Most verbs need 'ed' at the end to make them into the past tense.

dance ⟶ He danc<u>ed</u>   We agree ⟶ We agree<u>d</u>

Add 'd' to the end if the verb already ends in 'e'.

Some past tense verbs are **different**, for example:

catch ⟶ caught   buy ⟶ bought   teach ⟶ taught   think ⟶ thought

Some verbs don't change at all in the past tense. ⟶ put   cut   let   set

There are Two Main Ways to Talk About the Future

- You can talk about **future actions** by using '**am**', '**is**' or '**are**' with the verb 'going'.

  I am going to watch the match.   We are going to watch the match.

  Always use a verb with 'to' in front of it after 'going'.

- You can use '**will**' with a present tense verb.   He will sing.

Now Try This

1) Draw lines to match each sentence to the correct tense.

I will meet you at the café in town.		Present tense
We walked to the bar.		
		Past tense
He visits the dentist.		
She knew the way home.		Future tense

Section One – Using Grammar

Using Tenses

2) Tick the box next to the sentence that is in the **present tense**.

   My boss called me earlier this morning. ☐

   Alana's friend will go on holiday in two weeks. ☐

   Steve talks to his grandparents about his day. ☐

3) Rewrite each pair of sentences to be about the time given.

   a) (the **past**)

   I am developing my communication skills and working hard to be a better speaker.
   I am also attending a course that will increase my confidence.

   ....

   ....

   ....

   b) (the **present**)

   Matthew built a rabbit hutch with his nephew and niece. He taught the
   children how to use a range of different tools and how to work safely.

   ....

   ....

   ....

   c) (the **future**)

   My two dogs compete in a local agility competition.
   They enjoy running around, so they have a wonderful time.

   ....

   ....

   ....

Notes

Using Verbs Correctly

You need to make sure that your verbs agree with the person or thing doing the action.

Verbs Need to Agree with Their Subject

Who You Are Writing About Changes Verbs

- You often need to add '**s**' or '**es**' when writing about a '**he**', a '**she**' or an '**it**'.

    he walk**s**   it move**s**   Katie rush**es**

You Need to Use 'Is' and 'Are' Correctly

Rebecca **is** flying to Australia.
You should use 'is' when writing about one person or thing.

Rebecca and Gabs **are** flying to Australia.
You should use 'are' when writing about more than one person or thing.

'Have' and 'Has' Go with 'Been' or 'Done'

I **have been** waking up early this week.

She **has done** her weekly budgeting.

You can't miss out the verbs 'have' or 'has' from these sentences — they won't make sense without them.

Don't confuse 'have' with 'of' — they sound similar but are different words.

It's Easy to Confuse 'Don't' with 'Doesn't'

- **Don't** means 'do not'. ➡ Use 'don't' with 'I', 'you', 'we' and 'they'.
- **Doesn't** means 'does not'. ➡ Use 'doesn't' with 'he', 'she' and 'it'.

Now Try This

1) Circle the correct verb in each sentence below.

   a) We **is** / **are** going to the shops later.

   b) I will **mixes** / **mix** these paints.

   c) You **brought** / **brings** crisps to the party.

   d) He **is** / **are** my colleague.

2) Rewrite the verb in bold from each of the sentences below so that it **agrees** with the subject.

   a) Brett **wash** the dinner dishes most nights. ....

   b) She **close** her store for lunch every day. ....

Using Verbs Correctly

3) Rewrite the following sentences so that they use verbs correctly.

   a) Adi don't have her driving licence yet.

   ....

   b) Adi does has her provisional licence.

   ....

   c) Patrick support his brother whenever he dance in competitions.

   ....

   d) Isobel and Stephen is looking forward to watching my band performs live.

   ....

4) Rewrite the forum post below so that it uses verbs correctly.

   Andrei Novak
   6h ago   Forum Member

   Hello. I'm frustrated because I has been trying to put up a shelf, and it won't sits straight. The instruction book don't have any useful information. Can anyone help me?

   ....
   ....
   ....

Notes

Modal Verbs

These pages will help you get to grips with modal verbs and how to use them in your writing.

Modal Verbs are Always Used with Other Verbs

Modal Verbs Change the Meaning of a Sentence

Modal verbs come **before** the **main verb** of a sentence. Here are the **main** modal verbs:

| can | could | may | might | shall | should | will | would | must |

They show:

- how **likely** something is   I **might** learn Swahili.   The word 'might' suggests there is a small chance.

- your **ability** to do something   I **can** speak French.   The word 'can' shows that it is possible.

- whether you **need** to do something.   You **must** learn a new language.   The word 'must' shows that it is necessary.

You Can Turn Modal Verbs into Negatives

| can't | couldn't | shouldn't | won't | wouldn't | mustn't |

The examples of negatives above are informal.

The **formal** versions of these words should be written in full, e.g. '**could not**' or '**must not**'.

Now Try This

1) Tick the boxes next to the **three** sentences describing the actions that are **most likely** to happen.

   I must mow the grass this weekend. ☐

   Bethany could have become a professional footballer. ☐

   He will leave the office early today. ☐

   Virat ought to decide what to make for dinner this week. ☐

   Dolma is a Turkish dish that can be served hot or cold. ☐

   I shall call you after I finish cooking my dinner. ☐

Modal Verbs

2) Draw lines to match each sentence to the correct modal verb or phrase.

Vlad ... arrived by now.   will

Each modal verb only links to one sentence.

Kal, ... I borrow the book after you?   should have

Sharon ... catch the train if she runs.   may

3) Use the word bank to complete each sentence below. Use each word once.

wouldn't   could   should   won't

a) Tyrone knew he .... rest, but he tidied his house instead.

b) I .... use that computer if I were you: it's not working properly.

c) .... you feel cold without a jacket?

d) I .... be a bit late to the party, so save me some cake!

4) Write **one** sentence of your own for each of the modal verbs below.

might   mustn't   shall

1 ....

2 ....

3 ....

Notes

Grammar Practice

It's time to practise what you've learned in this section by working through these grammar questions.

Correct Grammar Makes Sentences Easier to Understand

Double-check Your Grammar to Make Sure It's Correct

Checking your grammar will help you make your sentences **clear**.

Here are the key points to keep in mind:

- A sentence must **make sense** on its own.
- Sentences use **tenses** to show **when** something happens.
- Verbs need to **agree** with the **subject** of a sentence.
- Modal verbs describe **ability**, **necessity** or **possibility**.

Look back at pages 4-11 for more on these topics.

Now Try This

1) Tick the boxes next to the **two** sentences that are grammatically correct.

   I think that my train today are cancelled. ☐

   Tamara's holiday starts tomorrow and she hasn't made any plans. ☐

   David felt certain that he'd locked his front door. ☐

   I have an meeting at later this afternoon. ☐

2) Circle the incorrect verb in each sentence and write a correction on the line.

   a) They go grocery shopping yesterday . ...

   b) The bakery now have many employees . ...

   c) She don't have time to cook tonight . ...

   d) Kevin could have wakes up earlier . ...

Section One – Using Grammar

Grammar Practice

3) Rewrite each sentence, correcting the **one** mistake.

   a) Lizzie accidentally walked into an university building instead of the post office.

   ....

   b) My mum come over yesterday and helped me pack up my house.

   ....

   c) I always worn a seatbelt when I am a passenger in a car.

   ....

4) The text below contains **five** grammatical mistakes.

   > Pat is driving home from work when an warning light comes on in his car. He decides it probably don't matter, and keeps driving. After a few minutes, his car slows down and stops in the middle of the road. He calls the local garage and they come to collects him. Pat should of taken his car for a service last week. He won't made that mistake again.

   Rewrite the text and **correct** the mistakes.

   ....

   ....

   ....

   ....

   ....

   ....

Notes

Section Two – Using Correct Punctuation

Using Commas

Commas can be used in lots of different ways — so make sure you know what they are.

Commas Affect the Structure of a Sentence

Commas Can Separate Items in a List

I bought a dress, a hat, some trousers and a pair of socks.

Put a comma after each thing in the list. Between the last two things you don't need a comma — use 'and' or 'or' instead.

Commas can break up lists of three or more things.

Commas Can Join Two Points

I wanted to bake a cake, but I didn't have any flour.

Joining words are words like 'and', 'so' and 'but'.

Two sentences can be joined together by using a comma and a joining word.

Commas Can Separate Extra Information

My colleague, Ashna, is covering my shift tomorrow.

Extra details might tell you things like 'who', 'which', 'whose', 'when' or 'where'.

Extra information should be inside the commas.

The sentence should make sense with or without the extra information.

Now Try This

1) Draw lines to match each sentence to how it uses commas.

I should eat healthily, yet I still eat a lot of chocolate.

My father, who works at a school, lives next door.

I have lived in Manchester, Amsterdam and London.

She ate her lunch, which was a tuna sandwich, in the park.

Katie wants to go on holiday, so she's saving money.

To separate items in a list

To join two points

To separate extra information

Using Commas

2) Correct each sentence by putting commas in the right places.

   a) My daughter likes to watch comedies dramas and musicals.

   b) I need a sofa two cushions a chair and a television for my new flat.

   c) He has a pint of milk three carrots a carton of eggs and some cheese.

   d) My uncle cousin brother and niece are coming to stay with us.

3) Rewrite each pair of sentences as a **single sentence** using a comma and **one** of the joining words below. Use each joining word once.

   so   or   yet

   a) People should exercise regularly. Most people do not have enough spare time.

   ....
   ....

   b) You can watch films at home. You can watch films in the cinema.

   ....
   ....

   c) It is raining outside today. Make sure you remember to take an umbrella.

   ....
   ....

4) Add **two commas** to each sentence to separate the extra information.

   a) My sister who works in a hospital is called Penny.

   b) I arrived at the house the biggest building in town around midday.

Notes

Colons and Lists

You probably won't need to use many colons in your writing, but they come in handy from time to time.

Colons Are Used to Introduce Things

- Colons can introduce an **explanation** → She wanted to celebrate: she'd passed her test.

- Colons can introduce **a quotation** → He told me: "Never give up on your dreams."

- Colons can introduce **a list** → I wrote three things: a poem, a letter and a play.

Colons Follow Several Rules

Don't use a capital letter after a colon, unless the word is a proper noun (e.g. *London*).

The writing before a colon must be closely linked to the writing after the colon.

The writing before a colon must make sense on its own.

Now Try This

1) Tick the box next to each sentence that uses a colon correctly.

   Jeremy needs to go home immediately: he isn't feeling well. ☐

   I need two things: from the shop a sponge and some soap. ☐

   Piotr screamed loudly he had spotted a spider: on the wall. ☐

   The security guard repeated his message: "We're closed today." ☐

   She introduced her three cousins: Michael, Jacob and Rebecca. ☐

2) Correct each sentence by putting a colon in the right place.

   a) Linda studied as much as she could she wanted to become a nurse.

   b) I'm not going on holiday this year I need to save some money.

   c) Fatimah is busy tomorrow evening she is going to a yoga class.

   d) I am trying to find a postbox I need to post a card to my aunt.

   e) Jonathan needs some kitchen scales he is planning on baking a cake.

Colons and Lists

3) Rewrite each sentence below, putting a colon in the right place.

   a) My teacher gave me some advice "Check your answers at the end of the exam."

   ....

   ....

   b) The book starts with a description of the weather "It was a wet and windy day."

   ....

   ....

4) Correct each sentence by putting a colon in the right place.

   a) I have errands to do later I must tidy my flat and return a parcel.

   b) My wife bought some tools an electric drill a hammer and a saw.

   c) We passed some sights on our journey a field of sheep and a waterfall.

5) Read the menu below.

   Benny's Bistro — Menu

   Food options available:
   - Vegetable bake
   - Cottage Pie
   - Soup
   - Sandwiches

   Remember to use correct punctuation when rewriting the sentence.

   Rewrite the menu as a full sentence that uses a colon.

   ....

   ....

Notes

Apostrophes

Apostrophes may be small but they can be easy to misuse, so make sure you know how to use them.

Apostrophes Often Make Sentences Shorter

Apostrophes Show That Letters are Missing

- Apostrophes can show where letters have been **removed**.

    She is ⟶ She's   We are ⟶ We're   I am ⟶ I'm

Apostrophes Show Something Belongs to Someone

- Apostrophes can show that someone **owns** something.

    The cat belonging to Charlotte ⟶ Charlotte's cat

- The apostrophe should go **after** the '**s**' if the noun is a word that **already ends** in '**s**'.

    Chris' pen   Alexis' bed   the octopus' tank   the doctors' meetings

    If a plural ends in 's', you still add an apostrophe to the end of the word.

- If a plural **doesn't end** in '**s**', add an **apostrophe** and '**s**'.

    We celebrated International Women's Day

Know the Difference Between It's and Its

It's almost time for us to go home.   The dog wagged its tail excitedly.

It's with an apostrophe means **it is** or **it has**.   **Its** without an apostrophe means **belonging to it**.

Now Try This

1) Rewrite each sentence, shortening the bolded words by using an apostrophe.

Sentence	Sentence with apostrophe
I **should not** have been late.	I shouldn't have been late.
It **is not** very sunny today.	....
Who is going to leave?	....
I wish **you had** called earlier.	....

Apostrophes

2) Fill in the gaps to explain **who** each object **belongs** to. The first one has been done for you.

   a) Samuel has a blue phone. → Samuel's phone is blue.

   b) Alice has a coat on the chair. → That is .... coat on the chair.

   c) Martin has a broken laptop. → .... laptop is broken.

3) Tick **one** box for each sentence below to show if the word in bold is singular or plural.

	Singular	Plural
a) The **cat's** whiskers twitched.	☐	☐
b) I walked into the **managers'** meeting.	☐	☐
c) **Jess'** dance shoes are brand new.	☐	☐
d) The **employees'** workplace is being cleaned.	☐	☐

   'Singular' means that there is only one of something. 'Plural' means more than one.

4) Draw lines to match each sentence below to the correct description of the word in bold.

   The car was missing **its** wheels.

   Where are the **men's** toilets?   Plural

   The **people's** house is huge.   Possessive

   The **girl's** leg is broken.   Plural and possessive

   We saw some **ladies** singing.

5) Write a sentence that includes **one possessive** apostrophe and **one plural**.

   ....

Notes

# Inverted Commas and Quotation Marks

We're almost done with punctuation, I promise. Just inverted commas and quotation marks to go...

Inverted Commas and Quotation Marks Come in Pairs

Inverted Commas and Quotation Marks Are Similar

Both inverted commas and quotation marks go at the **start** and the **end** of a word or phrase.

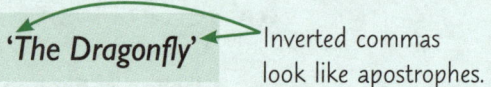 Inverted commas look like apostrophes.

 Quotation marks look like two apostrophes.

Inverted Commas Are Used for Titles

- Single inverted commas go at the start and end of **titles**, like the names of films or books.

  I bought 'Trading Explained' from the bookshop.   'Moonstar' is my favourite film.

Quotation Marks Are Used to Quote

- Quotation marks, also known as double inverted commas, are used to report **exactly** what was said.
- Quoted speech needs to be **punctuated correctly**:

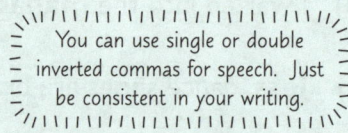
You can use single or double inverted commas for speech. Just be consistent in your writing.

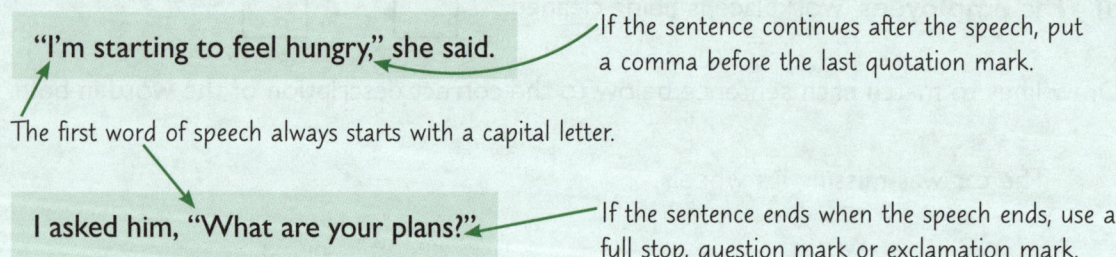

"I'm starting to feel hungry," she said. — If the sentence continues after the speech, put a comma before the last quotation mark.

The first word of speech always starts with a capital letter.

I asked him, "What are your plans?" — If the sentence ends when the speech ends, use a full stop, question mark or exclamation mark.

Now Try This

1) Correct each sentence below by putting **single inverted commas** in the right places.

   a) The doctor spent the evening reading Medical Matters Magazine .

   b) This is my first time watching an episode of Winthrop Mansion .

   c) I brought a copy of The Bullfrog Chronicles when I went camping .

2) Correct each sentence below by putting **quotation marks** in the right places.

   a) I'm going to the supermarket after I finish work, he said .

   b) On my walk to town I said Good morning! to the postman .

   c) I asked the waiter, Can I have the bill please ? He said, Of course .

Inverted Commas and Quotation Marks

3) Rewrite these sentences, putting **quotation marks** and **other punctuation** in the right places.

   a) Ravi replied I'm not hungry

   ....

   b) Congratulations cheered the crowd

   ....

4) Tick the boxes next to the sentences that are punctuated correctly.

   The article 'Prison Life' was eye-opening. ☐

   One journalist asked, "Are taxes being increased"? ☐

   "Remember to bring a bag!" shouted my colleague. ☐

   I used to love the film The Girl and the Kangaroo. ☐

5) Read the following part of a review.

   > Last week, I went to go and see the new film The Island of Yesterday.
   >
   > Film critic Ali Winterson, writing for The Cinema Gazette, said, I absolutely loved it.

   Rewrite the text putting **quotation marks** and **inverted commas** in the right places. Add in other punctuation where it is needed.

   ....

   ....

   ....

   ....

Notes

Punctuation Practice

The last few pages covered a lot of punctuation. Now it's time to put all that knowledge into practice.

Each Punctuation Mark Has a Specific Purpose

Try Not to Mix Up the Different Punctuation Marks

Using the **correct punctuation** in the **correct places** is an important part of the Writing exam. Here's a quick reminder of what each of these different punctuation marks do:

- **Commas** → can **separate** items in a **list**, **join** two points or separate **extra information**.
- **Colons** → can **introduce** an explanation or quotation.
- **Apostrophes** → can show **missing letters** or that something **belongs** to someone.
- **Inverted commas** → used for **titles** or **speech**.
- **Quotation marks** → used to **quote speech**.

Now Try This

1) Draw lines to match each sentence to the punctuation it is missing.

   a) The shop wont open until tomorrow morning. — Comma

   b) I need two things a bottle of water and a snack. — Inverted commas

   c) Piotr was wearing a red blue and purple jumper. — Colon

   d) He watched an episode of Penelope's Farm. — Apostrophe

   Now write each sentence, putting the missing punctuation in the correct place.

   a) ....

   b) ....

   c) ....

   d) ....

Punctuation Practice

2) Circle the correct option in each sentence below.

   Sharon and Patek adopted two **hamster's / hamsters** at the weekend.

   Maryam loved the fit of the dress but did not like **it's / its** colour.

   Sara told me that the **women's / womens'** basketball class begins in an hour.

   James's / James' new job is located on the outskirts of town.

3) Correct each sentence below by putting **punctuation** in the correct places.

   Jupiter is the largest planet in our solar system he explained .

   Marcus sister is going to see The Toxic Tree at the cinema .

   I saw Jennifer my brothers neighbour at the zoo last week .

4) The diary entry below contains **six** punctuation mistakes:

   17th September 2024
   I started reading a book called The Inn on the Sea' today.
   Its been quite boring so far: the main characters plan is really predictable.
   In the afternoon, I called two people Leanne and Chidi. I havent got any plans
   for this evening yet. Tomorrow, I need to bake a cake buy a card,
   wrap presents and visit my grandmother.

   Rewrite the diary entry using the correct punctuation.

   ....

   ....

   ....

   ....

Notes

Section Three – Using Correct Spelling

Spelling Rules and Plurals

There are marks for spelling in your writing assessment, so make sure to memorise these rules.

You Should Learn These Spelling Rules

Use the 'i' Before 'e' Rule

The 'i' before 'e' rule helps you to know which letter comes first.

'i' before 'e' except after c, but only when it rhymes with 'bee'.

For example:

bel**ie**ve	rec**ei**ve	w**ei**ght	sc**ie**nce
No 'c', rhymes with 'bee'	'c', rhymes with 'bee'	No 'c', doesn't rhyme	'c', doesn't rhyme

Watch out — some tricky words **don't** follow this rule:

c**ei**ling ← 'e' put before 'i' that rhymes with bee. → caff**ei**ne   'i' put before 'e', even though it comes after 'c' and rhymes with bee. → spec**ie**s

Plural Means 'More Than One'

To talk about more than one of something, usually you add an 's'.
Plurals can be spelt in different ways depending on how the word ends:

Word ends in:	How you usually make the plural form:
Consonant then 'y'	Turn the '**y**' into an '**i**' and add '**es**'. E.g. one lady, two ladies.
Vowel then 'y'	Add an '**s**'. E.g. one key, two keys.
'ch', 'x', 's', 'sh', 'z', 'o'	Add an '**es**'. E.g. one glass, two glasses.
'f' or 'fe'	Change the '**f**' to a '**v**' and add '**es**'. E.g. one half, two halves.

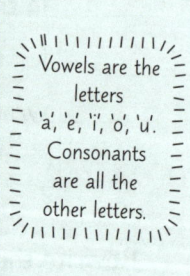
Vowels are the letters 'a', 'e', 'i', 'o', 'u'. Consonants are all the other letters.

Some words **don't follow a pattern** when they become plural:

t**oo**th → t**ee**th   wom**a**n → wom**e**n   m**ou**se → m**i**ce

Now Try This

1) Circle the correct plural form in each sentence below.

   a) She bought two fresh **loafs** / **loaves** of bread to make sandwiches.

   b) They studied the behaviour of the **monkeys** / **monkies** at the local zoo.

   c) I need five **potatoes** / **potatos** for this recipe, but I only have three.

Spelling Rules and Plurals

2) Rewrite each word with the correct spelling.

   Reciept: ....   Wieght: ....   Freind: ....

   Acheive: ....   Thier: ....   Reveiw: ....

3) Write the plural for each of the following words.

   Fly: ....   Pass: ....   Play: ....

   Box: ....   Leaf: ....   Buzz: ....

4) Rewrite the following sentences with the correct spellings.

   a) The gate into the feild was breifly left open, and the sheep escaped.

   ....

   b) The local nature soceity gave a lecture about anceint oak trees.

   ....

5) Rewrite the following sentences with the correct plurals.

   a) Summer brings blue skys and long, sunny dayes.

   ....

   b) The thiefs stole all of the jewels from the boxs.

   ....

Notes

Using Prefixes and Suffixes

Prefixes and suffixes are added to the start or end of words — being able to spell them is important.

Prefixes and Suffixes Make New Words

Prefixes and suffixes are added to words to change their meaning.

Prefixes are Letters Added to the Start of Words

When you add a prefix, the spelling of the word doesn't change.

Some common prefixes are: ir-, im-, de-, dis-, un- and in-

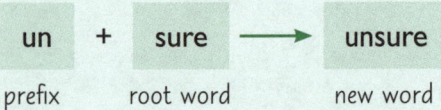

prefix   root word   new word

Suffixes are Letters Added to the End of Words

Adding a suffix might change the spelling.

If the root word ends with 'e' and the suffix starts with a vowel, you usually drop the 'e'.	If the root word ends with a consonant then a 'y', change the 'y' into an 'i'.
dare + ing → dar<u>i</u>ng	pre<u>tt</u>y + ness → pre<u>tti</u>ness

To add a suffix that starts with a **vowel**, use the **C-V-C** (consonant-vowel-consonant) rule. If the root word ends with C-V-C, you **double** the last letter when adding the suffix:

hop + ed → ho**pp**ed   sp**lit** + ing → spli**tt**ing

Don't double the last letter if the suffix starts with a **consonant**.

forget + ful → forgetful

Now Try This

1) Draw lines to match the words in the middle to the prefix and suffix that can be added to them to make a new word.

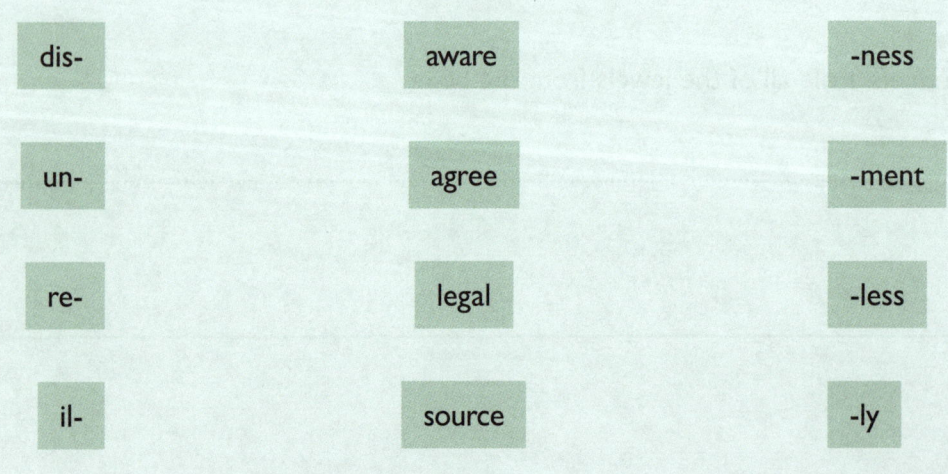

dis-	aware	-ness
un-	agree	-ment
re-	legal	-less
il-	source	-ly

Using Prefixes and Suffixes

2) Add each prefix to **one** of the words below to make **four** new words.

in- **im-** **un-** **ir-**

.... possible   .... effective   .... responsible   .... bearable

3) Add each suffix to **one** of the words below to make **four** new words.

-less **-ness** **-able** **-ly**

Careful ....   Good ....   Thought ....   Read ....

4) Circle the **four** words with incorrectly spelt suffixes in the text below.

> Staying cool in hot weather is extremely important. You must make sure you're wearring enough sun protection. This includes puting on enough suncream. There's nothing worse than getting a sunburn at the begining of a holiday! If you do get sunburnt, stay covered and keep your skin as hydrated as you can. Suny weather is great, but take care out there!

Write the correct spelling of each word on the lines below.

a) ....   b) ....

c) ....   d) ....

5) Use **each** of the following prefixes and suffixes once:

dis- **un-** **-ly** **-ful**

....
....

Notes

Words That Are Often Misspelt

Some tricky words can't be spelled using a rule — in these cases it's best to memorise them.

Learn How to Spell Tricky Words

Double Letters Aren't Always Obvious

Learn these common words with double letters:

| Di**ff**erent | Tomo**rr**ow | A**dd**re**ss** | Immediate |
| Pro**f**essional | Su**cc**e**ss** | Nece**ss**ary | O**cc**asionally |

Look Out for Silent Letters

Some words have letters that you **can't hear** when you say them out loud...

W**h**en | Dou**b**t | **W**rite | **K**now | Coul**d**

Learn these examples of words with silent or unclear letters.

... or contain letters that can't be heard clearly:

Bec**a**use | Defin**i**tely | D**e**scribe | Int**e**resting | Bus**i**ness

Some Words Are Mistaken for Others

To means 'towards' or is part of a verb.
Too can mean 'too much' or 'also'.

You're means 'you are'.
Your means 'belonging to you'.

'A lot' is two words. Don't write 'alot' — it's incorrect.

They're means 'they are'.
Their means 'belonging to them'.
There refers to a place.

Maybe means 'perhaps'.
May be means 'might be'.

Off can mean 'away'.
Of is a linking word.

Now Try This

1) Circle the correct spelling in each sentence below.

   a) There is an **apointment** / **appointment** available next Tuesday.

   b) We can talk **tomorrow** / **tommorrow** if that's more convenient.

   c) There were three **differant** / **different** vegetarian options on the menu.

   d) Inside the **bilding** / **building** the air was much cooler.

   e) The students had brought **they're** / **their** notebooks to class.

Words That Are Often Misspelt

2) The following words are each missing **one** silent letter. Rewrite them correctly.

Handriting: ....

Scedule: ....

Nowledge: ....

Shoud: ....

3) Each sentence below contains **two** spelling mistakes. Rewrite the sentences with the **correct** spellings.

a) Can you discribe the dificulties you are having with your computer?

....

b) All the lights in the scool have been turned of.

....

c) He didn't lisen to my directions as he turned onto the rong road.

....

d) Give reception a call — are staff will be able too help you.

....

e) We are looking for people with previus office experiance.

....

f) The twins saw that there business was a huge succes with the townspeople.

....

Notes

Section Four – Structure and Planning

Audience and Purpose

The audience and purpose of any text you write will determine the type of language and tone you use.

You Need to Know Your Audience and Purpose

Your Audience is Who You are Writing For

- You should write **formally** if you are writing for a **professional** audience or someone you **don't know**.

See pages 52-53 for more about formality.

- Sometimes your audience is obvious:

  The audience of a newspaper article is 'people who read the newspaper'.

- Sometimes your audience is less obvious:

  The audience of a charity advert might be people who have free time to volunteer, items to donate or money to contribute — or all three.

Your Purpose is Why You are Writing

- How you write will **change** depending on what you want your writing to do.

- Your purpose might be:

to **inform**	to **persuade**	to **describe**
e.g. use facts	e.g. use emotive language	e.g. use lots of adjectives

Now Try This

1) Draw lines to match each type of text to the correct purpose.

   A scientific article — to explain

   A fictional short story — to instruct

   A manual for building a desk — to entertain

2) Complete the table below. The first row has been done for you.

Scenario	Audience	Purpose
An email updating family about a holiday	Family	to inform
A letter of complaint asking for a holiday refund		
A review on a hotel's website		

Audience and Purpose

3) Identify the audience and purpose of the text below.

> The most important part of painting a room is the preparation. It's tempting to skip these steps, but they're crucial if you want the perfect finish on your walls. If you're not confident with paintbrushes yet, put masking tape on skirting boards and door frames to avoid any accidents.

Audience: .... Purpose: ....

4) Write **two** sentences for each situation described below.
   Make sure your writing has an appropriate audience and purpose.

   a) A notice to your local community about an upcoming bake sale.

   ....
   ....
   ....

   b) A note telling a friend how to look after your dog while you're away.

   ....
   ....
   ....

   c) A letter asking your manager for a pay rise.

   ....
   ....
   ....

Notes

Organising Your Writing

Keeping your writing organised will make your text easier to follow and understand.

Layout Features Organise Your Writing

The way you lay out your writing can help to guide people through it.
A clear layout can also help you keep your thoughts organised and your points clear.

Structure Your Writing Sensibly

A → **How to Attract Birds to Green Spaces**

B → Setting up bird feeders

C → 1) Decide what types of bird you want to bring to the area.
2) Research what food those birds prefer.
3) Buy the correct bird feeder for that kind of food and set it up.

D ↓

Organisational feature	Purpose
A Heading	To tell the reader what your text is about.
B Subheading	To tell the reader what a section of your text is about.
C List (Numbered / Bullet point)	To break up information and put instructions in order.
D Table	To organise information clearly.

These features can be used in a range of text types, but you don't always have to include them all. Different texts usually require different features.

Now Try This

1) Write a heading for **each** of the following texts.

   a) A positive review of a coffee shop.

   ....

   b) A newspaper report about a new gym opening.

   ....

Section Four – Structure and Planning

Organising Your Writing

2) Read the following text.

> **Update on New Tram Service**
>
> Eyreburgh's long-awaited tram service will be opening next month. Travellers are advised to study the route maps and the timetable.
> There are four routes, which will cover the following areas: Martmont, Burnsfield, Levinstone and Baymarket.
>
> The trams will run every hour from 6 am, except for weekends when they will start at 8 am. They will run until midnight on weekdays, until 11 pm on Saturdays and until 10 pm on Sundays. Bank holiday timetables are not yet confirmed.

a) Pick out useful information from the first paragraph and write it in a **bullet point list**.

b) Suggest a **subheading** for the second paragraph.

3) Write your own short announcement or notice below.
It should include a heading, a subheading and either a numbered list or a table.

Notes

Using Paragraphs

Learning how and when to separate your writing will help you group information sensibly.

Paragraphs Break Your Writing Up

A paragraph is a group of sentences that talk about the same topic. Using paragraphs makes your writing easier to read by **dividing it** into smaller parts.

Use Paragraphs to Show a Change

Start a new paragraph when you write about a new **topic**, **person**, **place** or **time**. To start a new paragraph, start a new line and leave a space at the beginning.

Paragraphs are usually longer than one or two sentences.

The house at Ashmuir Park was designed in 1709 by the French architect Charles Verlay. It took several decades to build due to unexpected complications. When it was finally finished, the Monton family moved in.

The first sentence of a paragraph usually introduces the topic.

Paragraphs should be in a logical order. These paragraphs are ordered by date.

Ashmuir House remained a family home until 1972, when it was gifted to a charity and converted into a care home. Since then, it has been a valuable part of our community.

You can also leave a whole line free between paragraphs. This is often done in online writing.

Leave a space to show a new paragraph.

The gardens at Ashmuir were opened to visitors in 2001...

- You will lose marks if you don't use paragraphs in your writing assessment.

Now Try This

1) Tick the boxes next to the situations where you should start a new paragraph.

   Your story starts describing a time hundreds of years ago. ☐

   A new character starts talking to your main character. ☐

   You add an example to make your topic more interesting. ☐

   You describe a location you haven't mentioned before. ☐

   You've written more than three lines of text. ☐

Using Paragraphs

2) Read the text about Evgenia Petrova below.
   In the boxes on the right give a reason why each new paragraph has been started.

> Evgenia Petrova moved from Sofia, in Bulgaria, to a small town in Kent. She is a teaching assistant at a secondary school. She loves working with young people and coaches the school netball team twice a week.
> When she isn't working or coaching, Evgenia enjoys wild swimming. She often goes for an early morning swim in a nearby lake before going to work.
> Next summer, Evgenia is planning on taking a course to qualify as a lifeguard. She hopes to start a wild swimming club for people in the local community to join.

....

....

....

3) Write your own extended piece of writing using at least three paragraphs.

....
....
....
....
....
....
....
....
....
....

Notes

Section Four – Structure and Planning

Developing Sentences

Joining your ideas together correctly will help your writing move smoothly from point to point.

Joining Words Develop Your Writing

Use Joining Words to Add More Detail

- Different parts of a sentence can be connected using joining words. The words below can be used to join **two separate** sentences together:

  | for | and | nor | but | or | yet | so |

  Nate likes tennis, **but** Bea likes rugby.

  The words 'but' and 'or' can be used to show a difference or disagreement.

- Other joining words can be used to connect the **main** part of a sentence to a **less important** part:

  | until | although | if | because | while | after |

  I enjoy cooking **because** I love good food.

  'because I love good food' is an extra detail and doesn't make sense on its own.

  Don't overuse joining words — too many can make a sentence long and harder to follow.

Joining Words Can Help Structure Your Writing

| firstly | secondly | finally | however | therefore | for example |

The words 'firstly' and 'finally' can be used to introduce and conclude an argument.

'therefore' can be used to explain something in more detail.

Now Try This

1) Circle the correct joining word in each sentence below.

   a) I can't eat the biscuits **for** / **and** I'm allergic to nuts.

   b) It was raining **so** / **for** Emma took an umbrella.

   c) They waited for the parcel **but** / **nor** it never arrived.

2) Draw lines to match each sentence to the missing joining word. *Each joining word links to one sentence.*

   We won't buy any furniture _____ we move in.   although

   We had to take the bus _____ the train broke down.   until

   We're still friends _____ we don't see each other often.   because

Section Four – Structure and Planning

Developing Sentences

3) Rewrite each sentence below using the correct joining word. Use each word once.

before   if   yet   so   because

a) Dried chilli flakes will do .... you can't find fresh chillies.

b) I bought blue shoes .... that's my favourite colour.

c) They loved the campsite, ... they booked to go back next year.

d) We searched the beach for six hours .... we found my missing ring.

e) I don't like following recipes, ... I love cooking my own dishes.

4) Write **one** sentence that uses each joining word given.

a) (while): ....

b) (therefore): ....

c) (but): ....

d) (yet): ....

e) (nor): ....

Writing That Flows

This page is about how your writing fits together — it should be sensibly sequenced and streamlined.

Link Your Ideas Together

Writing that flows is **easy to follow** and moves smoothly from one point to the next.

Use Joining Words to Structure Your Writing

You can use joining words to:

See page 36 for more about joining words.

- put your points in **order**

    Firstly, we should...   Secondly, I want to...   Finally, you must...

    These words introduce your point in order of importance.   This word can round off an argument.

- **develop** your writing

    Therefore...   Consequently...   Although...   However...

    These words explain a result.   These words can be used to disagree.

- add **examples**

    For example...   For instance...   Such as...

    These phrases can all be used to back up a point or introduce evidence.

Now Try This

1) Draw lines to match each word or phrase to what it does.

    Nevertheless

    Thirdly   Orders points

    Furthermore

                                         Develops a point

    As a result

    Lastly   Introduces an example

    To demonstrate

Writing That Flows

2) Use 'Therefore', 'For example' and 'However' to complete the sentences below.

   a) Mitko works very hard. .... , he still makes time to enjoy himself.

   b) There are many ways to revise. .... , you can use flashcards.

   c) The car needs new tyres. .... , I am taking it to the garage.

   Now write one or two sentences of your own using at least one of the joining words above.

   ....

   ....

3) The bullet points below were written by someone describing their visit to a festival.

   - We arrived and collected our passes.
   - We found the campsite and pitched our tent.
   - We spent some time at the food stalls.
   - We went to watch some short performances.
   - We danced to our favourite artist at the main stage.

   Rewrite the points as a **paragraph** using appropriate words to put them in order. Keep the points in the same order.

   ....

   ....

   ....

   ....

Notes

Exciting Openings

The start of your writing sets the tone — it should be interesting and make people want to find out more.

Titles Should Grab People's Attention

A Title Should Be Informative and Engaging

- Your title should tell people what your writing is about.
- The **tone** of your title will **depend** on your audience, purpose and format:

Sausage Dog! Pet Eats £100 of Butcher's Stock

A light-hearted article may have a fun and informal title.

Not every text type needs a title — letters and emails have their own rules to follow.

An article about a serious issue is more likely to be formal. → **Local Lawyer Found Guilty of Fraud**

Opening Paragraphs Should Introduce the Topic

- Your **first sentences** should make it clear what you are writing about.
- The opening paragraph should be interesting to encourage people to continue reading.

This opening is engaging. → Ever fancied a night beneath the stars? Well, for two young hikers in the Lake District, they didn't have any other choice. After a long day in the hills, without a map or phone signal, they faced an evening in the wilderness with only sheep for company.

This tells us what the rest of the writing will be about.

Now Try This

1) Tick the boxes next to the **two** newspaper headlines that are the most attention-grabbing.

   How to Save More Energy at Home ☐

   Money Talks — Bribery Scandal Exposed ☐

   New Train Line Opens from Figton to Bimbleby ☐

   Britain Braces for a Sudden Storm ☐

2) Write a suitable headline for an article based on the introductory paragraph below.

   In a surprising turn of events, a long-standing Pinby bookshop, 'The Ink Trove', announced its sudden closure today, leaving many residents and customers shocked.

   ....

Exciting Openings

3) Draw lines to match each opening to the correct title.

| Searching for a fitness plan that's suitable for beginners? Look no further. | That's Bananas! |

| Forget the bustling tourist traps — here you'll find an authentic British coastal experience. | Employment Survey Results |

| Ms. Murray was weeding when she found an exotic plant growing in her garden. | Bawbury's Best Kept Secrets: A Local Guide |

| More Brits than ever are bringing in extra money with freelance jobs. | Get Moving — How To Be More Active This Summer |

4) For each text type and title below, write an opening paragraph to introduce the topic. Your paragraph should be **two to four** sentences long.

a) A blog post titled: 'My Morning Ritual: How I Start My Day'.

....
....
....
....

b) An article titled: 'The Impact of Technology on Catly Library'.

....
....
....
....

Notes

Powerful Conclusions

Writing conclusions can be tricky, but they are important — they reinforce the message of your writing.

A Conclusion Should Summarise Your Writing

Good Conclusions Are Memorable

No matter what type of text you're writing, it's always a good idea to include a conclusion.

A conclusion can include many techniques:

- I think everyone should try yoga. — *a summary or recommendation*
- Get on the phone and volunteer today! — *instructions or actions for people to take*
- Therefore, there are numerous benefits to this approach. — *a reminder / repetition of your main point*
- What are you waiting for? — *something thought-provoking, like a rhetorical question*

When writing a conclusion, you **should** also:

- Consider your **audience**. ← E.g. Don't become less formal later in your writing.
- Remember your **purpose**. ← E.g. Make sure you know why you are writing.

It's generally a good idea to keep conclusions clear and to the point.

Now Try This

1) Give the **purpose** of each conclusion below.

   a) The future of our town is in your hands — make sure you write to your local MP and let them know that things need to change.

   Purpose: ....

   b) In summary, it is so important for drivers to book their car's MOT in good time. Safe cars mean safer roads for everyone.

   Purpose: ....

   c) Overall, the food and atmosphere of this fantastic restaurant make it a must-visit for all locals and anyone visiting the area.

   Purpose: ....

Section Four – Structure and Planning

Powerful Conclusions

2) For the text type and title below, write a concluding paragraph.
   Your paragraph should be **two to four** sentences long and include a recommendation.

   a) A hotel review titled: 'Don't forget to do your research in advance'.

   ....
   ....
   ....
   ....

   b) A letter to the public titled: 'Support the high street before it's too late'.

   ....
   ....
   ....
   ....

   c) A newspaper article titled: 'Is radio old news? The rise of the podcast.'

   ....
   ....
   ....
   ....

Notes

Planning Your Answer

It's often useful to plan before you start writing — a good structure will help to get your point across.

A Plan Helps You Put Your Ideas in Order

A Plan Doesn't Need to be Perfect

- A plan doesn't need to be in full sentences — it won't be marked.
- Jot down any **key ideas** that you want to include — make sure they answer the question.
- **Organise** your ideas so that the most important ones come first.
- Work out your **audience** and **purpose** and note down how **formal** your writing will be.

Your plan could use bullet points or be in a table.

Use Your Plan to Write Your Answer

- Turn the points in your plan into full sentences.
- Use the same order and structure that you did in your plan.

Following a plan means you don't have to worry about the structure of your answer when you write it out.

Now Try This

1) The points below are from a plan for a job application cover letter. Write a number in each box to put the points in a sensible order.

   In summary — I'm a good fit for the role ☐

   I look forward to hearing from you soon ☐

   I'm writing to apply for the job advertised online ☐

   I have the necessary qualifications ☐

2) Turn the bullet points from the plan below into **two** full sentences.

   Weekend Picnic Plan

   Audience: your friends   **Purpose:** to inform

   - Everyone must bring food
   - Picnic blanket and suncream needed

   ....

   ....

   ....

Planning Your Answer

3) Imagine you are writing an article for a local newspaper that is **250-300** words long. Use the table below create a plan.

> You are informing local people about a new sports centre in town. Your article should encourage people to use the new centre.

You don't need to count exactly how many words you use — word counts are usually a rough guide.

Section	Content
Introduction	
Main Points	
Other points	
Any extra details	
Summary / Conclusion	

Now turn this plan into a full answer on a separate sheet of paper.

Notes

Checking and Correcting

Making a mistake in your writing isn't a problem as long as you know how to go back and correct it.

Improve Your Answers by Correcting Mistakes

Check Your Writing Carefully

Once you've finished writing your answers, **read through them**.

Look out for places where you might have:

- missed or misspelt a word
- repeated yourself
- made punctuation or grammar errors

Make sure you leave yourself enough time at the end of the assessment to look back over your answers.

Make Clear Corrections

- If you find a mistake, **cross it out** neatly. Write the correction **above** it:

    This careers fair is a good ~~oportunity~~ **opportunity** to meet useful contacts.

- Use two lines (//) to show where a **new paragraph** should start.

    ...from the restaurant. // On the second day, we visited the local art gallery.

- You can use the ∧ symbol to add in **one** word, or * to add in **more** than one:

    The website provides directions ∧**to** the hotel from the * bus station.
    * Oxenford Street

    This shows that you're adding in 'to' after 'directions'.

    The star here shows some words are missing.

    Use a star to show these are words you want to add. Add these words in the margin or at the bottom of the page.

Now Try This

1) There is **one** spelling mistake in each of the following sentences. Rewrite the misspelt word **correctly** in the box.

   a) Unfortunately, the fundraising event was very badly organnised. ....

   b) You can use the on line service to book an appointment. ....

   c) Everybody shoud be sitting down before the performance starts. ....

   d) The carpenter was inable to fix the broken table. ....

Section Four – Structure and Planning

Checking and Correcting

2) Read this travel brochure about visiting a town.
   Insert **two** '//' symbols to show where new paragraphs should start.

> Clarnton is a small town with plenty of interesting things to do and see. This includes boat rides, a museum of local history and an impressive clock tower.   The nearby village of Westing is worth a visit.   It is well-known for its excellent restaurants, with several different cuisines on offer. Visitors are encouraged to book tables ahead of time, as the restaurants in Westing are often busy.   In the summer months, there are plenty of activities available for those who want to try something outdoors — Tumnock Activity Centre is a good option.   From kayaking to nature walks, they have a great selection of activities to try, suitable for all ages.

3) The following email contains **three** spelling mistakes and **three** punctuation mistakes.
   Rewrite the email, correcting the mistakes.

> Hello Erin,
>
> Thank you for ofering to help us with the company dinner next week. Were organising transport for the helpers so if you'd like a lift to the restaurent please let me know.
>
> Do you have any allergies or dietary requirements The cook will need to now.
>
> All the best,
>
> Una

Notes

Section Five – Using the Right Language

Getting the Tone Right

The tone of your writing needs to be appropriate for your audience and the purpose.

The Tone of Your Writing Shows How You Feel

Tone Can Be Personal or Impersonal

- **Personal** writing involves your **point of view**.

  > I was shocked when I listened to the news.

  — This can include your opinions, feelings and experiences.

- **Impersonal** writing **doesn't** involve your **point of view**.

  > The news broadcaster explained the event.

  — Facts and straightforward language are used to explain the subject.

Tone Can Be Used to Show Emotion

> The sunset was a truly incredible sight!

A positive tone uses more upbeat language.

> I didn't enjoy the race as it was tough.

A negative tone uses less upbeat language.

Match Your Tone to Your Purpose

- Different **audiences** and **purposes** require **different** tones.
- An impersonal tone is more professional — making it useful for formal writing.
- A personal tone is more friendly — making it useful for informal writing.

Now Try This

1) Tick **one** box next to each scenario where a personal tone would be appropriate.

   An invitation to a birthday party. ☐

   A newspaper article about mortgages. ☐

   A blog post about childhood memories. ☐

2) Rewrite the following sentences with a more positive tone.

   a) "It's impossible to get a table at that restaurant."

   ....

   b) "I couldn't stand the hot weather — it was difficult to do anything."

   ....

Getting the Tone Right

3) Write a sentence using each of the tones given below.

   a) A personal and happy tone.

   ....

   b) A personal and worried tone.

   ....

   c) An impersonal tone.

   ....

4) Write an article about a local business that's becoming hugely successful. Use a formal and positive tone.

   ....
   ....
   ....
   ....
   ....
   ....
   ....
   ....

Notes

Writing Styles

A 'writing style' is how a text is written. Why you're writing (and who for) will affect your writing style.

Your Writing Style Should Match Your Purpose

Make Sure You Can Write in These Common Styles

Style	Purpose	What to Include
Advisory / Instructive	To tell someone what to do.	Simple language and command words, e.g. "should", "must", "ought to".
Descriptive	To help the reader imagine something.	Adjectives and emotive language.
Humorous	To entertain the reader.	Chatty language, imagery, exaggeration.
Explanatory / Informative	To tell the reader about a topic.	Facts and statistics, technical language.
Persuasive	To get the reader to agree with a point of view.	Adjectives, emotive language, language techniques.

- Sometimes you might need to use more than one style.

Now Try This

1) Draw lines to match each of the following texts to the style they are written in. *Each style links to one text.*

Text	Style
The Arts Centre will be closed on Monday night as there is an event taking place from 7 pm to 10:30 pm.	Descriptive
To get to the train station, turn left at the second set of traffic lights. Then keep going straight for about a mile.	Instructive
You should always check the weather forecast before you go on a long walk — especially if it's hot.	Persuasive
You'll not want to miss out on the best musical in town — final tickets are on sale now!	Explanatory
Our stay at the cottage was magical. The log fire was so comforting and we ate dinner by candlelight.	Advisory

Section Five – Using the Right Language

Writing Styles

2) Write **two** sentences using each prompt below.

   a) A persuasive advert encouraging people to buy a new phone.

   ....
   ....
   ....

   b) An advisory text telling people how to prepare for an interview.

   ....
   ....
   ....

3) Write **four** sentences to inform people on **one** of the following topics:

   A healthy morning routine.   How to make a simple meal.

   ....
   ....
   ....
   ....
   ....
   ....
   ....

Notes

Formal and Informal Writing

You'll need to know the situations when you should write formally and when you can write informally.

Your Formality Should Match Your Audience

Learn the Differences Between Writing Formally and Informally

- **Formal** writing sounds **professional** — it has an impersonal and serious tone.

  It uses precise, sometimes technical, language. → The board announced that they are in favour of postponing the conference, including the lectures, until the following week.
  - *It rarely uses contractions.*
  - *It uses complete sentences.*

- **Informal** writing sounds **personal** — it has a friendly and casual tone.

  It uses contractions. → Just thought I'd send you a quick update. I don't fancy going to the party later.
  - *It uses simple and usually short sentences.*
  - *It uses chatty, everyday language.*

Know When to Use Formal or Informal Writing

Different types of text or audience require different levels of formality.

- Formal writing is best for **professional** settings.
  E.g. *Emails to colleagues, job applications or newspaper articles.*
- Informal writing can be used in **casual** settings.
  E.g. *Messages to friends and family, personal blogs or social media posts.*

> If you're not sure how professional a piece of writing needs to be, it's usually best to write more formally.

Now Try This

1) For each of the following situations, tick **one** box to show whether formal or informal writing would be more appropriate.

		Formal	Informal
a)	An email to your manager.	☐	☐
b)	A letter to a close relative.	☐	☐
c)	A message to a senior colleague.	☐	☐
d)	A cover letter for a job application.	☐	☐

Section Five – Using the Right Language

Formal and Informal Writing

2) Read the following message to a technology company's recruitment team.

> Hi Megan,
>
> I figured I'd apply for the apprenticeship advertised on your company's website.
> Plus, I bet you'd have some advice about working in the tech industry and stuff.
> It'd be handy to chat with you about what I'd get up to in the role.
>
> Cheers,
> Alicia Horden

a) Underline any informal language.

b) Give **one** reason why this text should **not** use informal language.

....

c) Rewrite the message to use more appropriate language.

....
....
....
....
....
....
....
....

Notes

Giving Your Opinion

Sharing your opinions will be helpful in all sorts of writing — so make sure you know how to do it.

Opinions Tell People What You Think

You need to be able to write how you **feel** about something.

You can use these phrases to start writing an opinion:

I think...   I believe...   In my opinion...

Opinions are personal — other people might not share the same opinions that you have.

You Should Support Your Opinions

- When you give your opinion, it's often helpful to share your **reasoning**.
- Reasoning might include **facts** or your own **thoughts**. It can make your opinions easier for people to understand.

Reviews often share opinions.

I don't like cake.

This opinion states a preference without giving any reasoning.

I don't like cake — it's too sweet.

This opinion includes a reason — it's easier to understand why the opinion is held.

Consider Other People's Opinions

- Mentioning other people's opinions can make your writing seem more **balanced**.
- If people think your writing is fair, they're more likely to respond well to your opinions when you share them.

You still need to make your own opinion clear.

Now Try This

1) Underline any opinions in the passage below.

> There's a new roundabout in Dentham, and I find the lane going through the middle of it confusing. I don't think there are enough signs for the roundabout. There have already been two accidents. I strongly believe something should be done about this.

2) Which of the following opinions is best supported by its reasoning?

   a) Tick **one** box.

   "My football team is great: we've won three trophies." ☐

   "My football team is the best: they're excellent." ☐

   b) Then give **one** reason for your choice.

   Reason: ....

Section Five – Using the Right Language

Giving Your Opinion

3) Give your opinion on each statement below in **two** sentences.

   a) "Doing things quickly is more important than doing them perfectly."

   ....

   ....

   b) "Drivers should have to retake their driving test every ten years."

   ....

   ....

   c) "All shops should be open on a Sunday."

   ....

   ....

4) Give a **different** opinion on each topic below.   Include a reason for your opinion.

   "I think work uniforms are a waste of time."

   ....

   ....

   "In my opinion, online shopping is great."

   ....

   ....

Notes

Writing Persuasively

Writing persuasively means getting people to agree with you or do what you want — pretty useful.

Persuasive Writing Convinces People

Give People Reasons to Agree with You

Your writing **can't** just **tell** people to agree with you — you need to **explain why** they should.

"You should avoid this café **because** the cutlery is always filthy."

Persuasive writing is useful when writing reviews, adverts and arguments.

Involving Your Audience in Your Writing

- **A direct address** is when your writing talks directly to its audience.

    Words like 'you' and 'your' involve the audience. → You and your family will love our latest adventure day.

- **Rhetorical questions** are questions that don't need an answer. They are often used to make people agree with the writer.

    Do you care about saving abandoned pets? ← This question is written so that the only sensible answer is 'yes'.

Use Persuasive Language

Your writing should use appropriate techniques to persuade your audience.

- **Emotive Language**: Local charities are <u>desperate</u> for help. — The word 'desperate' will make people feel sorry for the charities.

- **Alliteration**: <u>B</u>illy's <u>B</u>argain <u>B</u>azaar — Repeating sounds at the start of words makes them catchy and memorable.

- **The Rule of Three**: I'm <u>sad</u>, <u>angry</u> and <u>disappointed</u>. — Listing three negative words emphasises this writer's feelings.

Now Try This

1) Which of the following statements is written persuasively?

   a) Tick **one** box.

   "Let's go to the nature reserve — it's full of fascinating creatures." ☐

   "Will you come to the cinema with me this weekend?" ☐

   b) Give **one** reason for your choice.

   Reason: ....

Section Five – Using the Right Language

Writing Persuasively

2) Write **one** persuasive sentence for each of the following scenarios.
   Use a different persuasive technique in each sentence.

   a) A positive review of a new restaurant.

   ....

   b) A comment complaining about roadworks in town.

   ....

   c) A positive description of a product for sale.

   ....

   d) A welcome slogan for a theme park.

   ....

3) Write a review persuading people to use a construction company.
   Include at least **three** different persuasive techniques in your writing.

   ....
   ....
   ....
   ....
   ....
   ....
   ....

Notes

Section Six – Using the Right Format

Writing Emails

When writing an email, it's important to follow a specific structure — make sure you lay it out correctly.

Match Your Style to Your Audience

Formal Emails are for Professional Purposes

- Emails to **companies**, people in positions of **authority** and people you **don't know** should be **formal**.
- Use 'Dear Sir / Madam' if you don't know the name of the person you're emailing.

Informal Emails are for More Casual Purposes

- With **friends and family**, your emails can be more **personal**.
- You can use **friendlier** greetings / sign-offs and include their **name**.

See pages 52-53 for more on formal and informal writing.

Use the Correct Layout for Emails

Send	To:	hobbs.maps@azmail.co.uk ← Recipient's email address.
	Subject:	Map-reading course ← What the email is about.

Dear Ms Hobbs, ← An appropriate greeting.

I am emailing to register my interest in your map-reading course next week. I would like to join the 6 pm group on Friday if possible. ← Use paragraphs to break up your points.

Please could you let me know if you still have spaces available?

Yours sincerely, ← An appropriate sign-off. Use 'Yours sincerely' if you know their name and 'Yours faithfully' if you don't.

Erika Cusk

Now Try This

1) Tick **one** box to show whether you should write a formal or informal email for each situation.

	Formal	Informal
a) Making a hotel reservation.	☐	☐
b) Asking a close friend for advice.	☐	☐
c) Booking a dentist appointment.	☐	☐
d) Sending a complaint to a company.	☐	☐

Writing Emails

2) Write an appropriate greeting and sign-off for each email below.

	Email	Greeting	Sign-off
a)	A complaint about a missing parcel to a Mr Cleveland.	....	....
b)	A message to your friend Cameron inviting them to a party.	....	....
c)	You're submitting a job application to a recruitment company.	....	....

3) Read the scenario below, then answer the question.

You work for Gaughcott Community Gym. An equipment delivery hasn't arrived. Write an email of around **50 words** to ask where the delivery is.

To: wesellweights.complaints@azmail.co.uk
Subject: Order number 224

....

....

....

....

....

....

....

Notes

Writing Letters

Letters are similar to emails, but they have some extra rules to follow when it comes to writing addresses.

Think About the Structure of Your Letter

Some Letters Can be Formal...

Many of the rules for letters and emails are the same.

- If you **don't know** the person you are writing to, your letter should be **formal**.
- Use 'Dear Sir / Madam' if you don't know the name of the person you're writing to.

... And Some Letters Can be Informal

- With **friends and family**, your letters can be more **personal**.
- You can use **friendlier** greetings / sign-offs and include their **name**.

Lay Letters Out Correctly

Put the name or title of the person you're writing to.

Write their full address.

Use their name if you know it.

Use paragraphs.

Use 'Yours sincerely' if you know their name and 'Yours faithfully' if not.

Regional Manager
Local Company
19 Bridge Street
Benchton, Derbyshire
EG12 0NT

Dear Sir / Madam,

I am writing to thank your company for its excellent service...

... Overall, I was very pleased with the work that was done.

Yours faithfully,

Ms Iris Milhaud

23 St. Margaret's Road
Lamberwell, Derbyshire
EG7 2AW

7th August

Write your address in the top right corner.

Include the date under your address.

Start by explaining why you're writing.

The main part of the letter would go here.

Use your full name for formal letters or your first name for informal letters.

Now Try This

1) Draw lines to show whether each letter should be formal or informal.

- A letter to your sister about a party.
- A letter to a tutor asking to hire them.
- A letter to a local politician about recycling.

Formal

Informal

Writing Letters

2) Read the following letter.

> Wilten Windows
> 36 Osten Close
> Marseydown, Warwickshire
> MR7 8FT
>
> Occupants
> 3 Banwell Street
> Marseydown, Warwickshire
> MR7 5BF
>
> Dear Sir / Madam,
>
> I'm writing to tell you about our new discounted window cleaning service covering Banwell Street and Catton Road.
>
> The service is available starting next month and the discount includes gutter cleaning.
>
> Best wishes.

a) Identify the **three** mistakes made in the letter.

1: ....

2: ....

3: ....

b) Write a letter in response to the one above, asking for more information.
Use the space below to plan your answer, then write it on a separate sheet of paper.

Notes

Writing Articles and Blogs

Make sure you're able to tell articles and blogs apart — they have a few key differences.

Articles and Blogs are Used to Explain Topics

Articles are Formal and Informative

- They are usually found in newspapers and magazines.
- They are written to **inform** or **explain** and often use facts.

Give your article a headline.

Your first paragraph introduces the topic.

Subheadings break up the text.

Use paragraphs to divide your points.

You can use quotes.

May use specialist words, which are only used to talk about specific subjects, e.g. the restaurant industry.

The last paragraph should be a summary or conclusion.

Blogs are Often More Personal

Blogs are found **online** and usually have a similar structure to articles. However:

- Blogs are more likely to contain personal opinions.
- Blogs often have a more **informal** tone than articles.

Now Try This

1) Circle the specialist word in each sentence below.

  a) The vet wrote up a detailed prescription for Posy's cat.

  b) Galina is learning how to use a kiln in her pottery class.

  c) Otters are excellent predators, despite being such small animals.

  d) Razvan has to check the shop's inventory every morning before he opens the doors.

Writing Articles and Blogs

2) Read the following text.

> **Wonderful Kestwick Wildlife**
>
> Last week I volunteered with Kestwick Wildlife Conservation. I helped to plant trees and clean up rubbish from footpaths.
>
> I found the whole experience really interesting and rewarding, and I definitely felt like I was making a difference.
>
> They're hoping for more volunteers next time, so give them a call!

a) Is the text more likely to be from an article or a blog? Circle your answer.

Article / **Blog**

Give **one** reason for your answer.

....

b) Write a short article about a charity that you support. Include the following:
- A headline
- Subheadings
- A specialist word

Use the space below to plan your answer, then write it on a separate sheet of paper.

Notes

Writing Reports

Reports can share lots of information, so it's important that you get the style and structure right.

Reports are Formal and Informative

Reports Should be Balanced

- Reports provide **information** about an issue.
- They analyse an issue before giving a **recommendation** or **summary**.

Reports often consider several sides of an issue.

Structure Reports Clearly

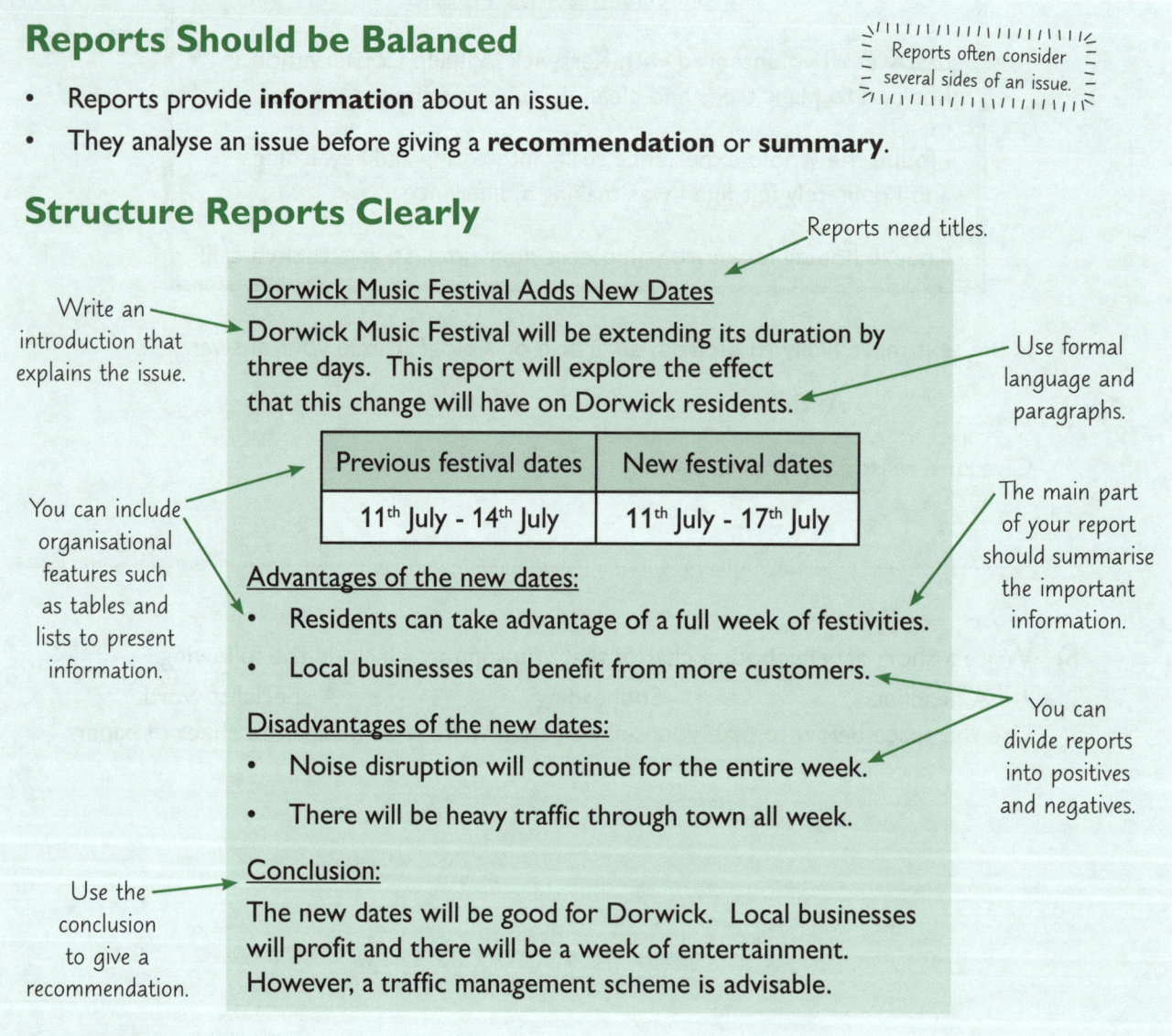

Reports need titles.

Write an introduction that explains the issue.

Dorwick Music Festival Adds New Dates

Dorwick Music Festival will be extending its duration by three days. This report will explore the effect that this change will have on Dorwick residents.

Use formal language and paragraphs.

Previous festival dates	New festival dates
11th July - 14th July	11th July - 17th July

You can include organisational features such as tables and lists to present information.

Advantages of the new dates:
- Residents can take advantage of a full week of festivities.
- Local businesses can benefit from more customers.

The main part of your report should summarise the important information.

Disadvantages of the new dates:
- Noise disruption will continue for the entire week.
- There will be heavy traffic through town all week.

You can divide reports into positives and negatives.

Conclusion:
The new dates will be good for Dorwick. Local businesses will profit and there will be a week of entertainment. However, a traffic management scheme is advisable.

Use the conclusion to give a recommendation.

Now Try This

1) Draw lines to match each of the following sentences to the part of a report they are from.

"Film fans should try the cinema in Newington instead."   Recommendation

"Local Cinema to Close for Refurbishment"   Introduction

"The cinema on Brunswick Street will close next month."   Title

Writing Reports

2) The bullet points below describe a shop's new range of waterproof trousers. Using the information given, write a short report about the product.

- The new trousers will be cheaper than the old version.
- The new trousers won't have the fleece-lining that the old version did.
- The new trousers will come in a wider range of materials and colours.

....

....

....

....

....

....

....

3) Summarise each of the following texts in **one** sentence.

a) In August, the road layout in Bay Grove is going to be updated. The plan is to build a roundabout on Lowe Street, where there is currently a four-way junction. This will create a smoother flow of traffic through the town.

....

b) If you're planning to visit Handleford Museum next month, be aware that ticket prices are changing. Children under 10 will still get in for free, but the price for an adult entry ticket is going up from £2.50 to £3.50. Their website has more information.

....

Notes

Writing Leaflets

Leaflets are often used to inform people about something — this could be an event, product or business.

Leaflets Can Be Informative and Persuasive

Leaflets Should Match Their Audience

- A leaflet might use formal language to **provide information** about a serious topic.

  Health and Safety at Work — What You Need to Know

- A leaflet might use chatty language to **persuade** people to do something.

  You're Invited to the Grand Opening of Skyhigh Theme Park!

Information sheets are similar to leaflets but are often more formal and may contain more facts.

Lay Out Leaflets Sensibly

Donate to Tilney Wharf Cat Shelter

Tilney Wharf Cat Shelter relies entirely on donations. Our costs are increasing and we need your help more than ever, so please consider donating.

What your donation will go towards:
- Buying cat food and cat litter.
- Keeping the shelter clean and tidy.
- Transport costs for our volunteers.
- Medication and vet treatment.

If you would like to make a donation, you can either visit the shelter or send us an email to arrange a bank transfer: tilneywharfcatshelter@azmail.co.uk.

- Give your leaflet a title.
- The first paragraph should summarise your leaflet.
- Use subheadings to make important information easier to find.
- You can use bullet points and numbered lists to break information up.
- This leaflet uses persuasive language to encourage people to donate.
- Include as much information as you can.

Now Try This

1) Tick **one** box to show the purpose of each sentence below.

	To inform	To persuade
a) "The local dentist is now accepting new patients."	☐	☐
b) "The museum gift shop opens at 9 am every day."	☐	☐
c) "Donating blood is a fantastic thing to do."	☐	☐
d) "The art gallery is the perfect weekend day out."	☐	☐

Section Six – Using the Right Format

Writing Leaflets

2) Rewrite each of the following sentences to be more persuasive.

   a) "Adopt a dog from a shelter."

   ....

   b) "Buy tickets to the charity concert."

   ....

   c) "Go to the new leisure centre."

   ....

3) A local nursing home is looking for new care assistants.
   Plan a leaflet which:

   • Gives information about the nursing home and what the job involves.
   • Persuades people to apply for the role.

   Use the space below to plan your answer, then write it on a separate sheet of paper.

Notes

Writing Adverts

Adverts are usually attention-grabbing and exciting — they make people feel or do something.

Adverts are a Type of Persuasive Writing

Adverts Should be Engaging

An advert usually tries to **convince** people to **do** something. Adverts often include:

- **Reasons** why people should do something.
- **Catchy** and **memorable** phrases.
- **Persuasive techniques**.
- A **friendly**, less formal **style**.

'Advert' is short for 'advertisement' — you should use the full word in formal writing.

See pages 56-57 for more on persuasive writing.

Adverts Should Look Attractive

Use catchy slogans to make adverts memorable.

A Fabulous New Flavour!
Try Fiza's Fantastic Fruit Juice, a dazzlingly delicious drink!

Language techniques like alliteration engage the reader.

What's not to love?
Imagine biting into a ripe and juicy piece of fruit on a summer's day. The sweet flavour bursts against your tongue as the golden sun warms your skin. That's how it feels to drink our juice.

Descriptive language helps people to imagine things.

Rhetorical questions can encourage the reader to agree.

Great taste, great for you!
Fiza's Fantastic Fruit Juice is fizzing with goodness. It's low in sugar and uses all natural ingredients, so it's both healthy and perfectly refreshing.

Give the reader a reason to do what you suggest.

Direct address makes the reader feel involved.

Now Try This

1) Write a catchy slogan for each of the following businesses.

   a) A hotel by the sea.

   ....

   b) A sports clothing company.

   ....

Section Six – Using the Right Format

Writing Adverts

2) Read the following sentences and name **one** persuasive technique used in each sentence.

   a) Treat yourself with a 20% discount on our delicious cupcakes.

   ....

   b) Want to discover the wonderful world of sea creatures?

   ....

   c) Here at Mop & Bucket, cleaning is our scene.

   ....

3) Write an advert for a company that organises hiking trips in the countryside.
   Use the space below to plan your answer, then write it on a separate sheet of paper.

Notes

Audience, Purpose and Tone

These questions are all designed to give you some extra practice with audience, purpose and tone.

1) Complete the table below. The first row has been done for you.

	Scenario	Audience	Purpose
	A leaflet advertising a new pantomime	Family	to persuade
a)	A cookie recipe		
b)	A hotel check-in email		
c)	A medical journal detailing new treatments		
d)	A collection of short stories		

2) Suggest a suitable **tone** for each piece of writing.

a) An email from a colleague thanking you for your help with a recent project.

b) A comic strip in a newspaper making fun of the weekly news stories.

c) A letter from the local council informing residents of new parking charges.

d) A leaflet inviting local people to a new social club at the village hall.

3) Write down **two** words that link to each tone below.

Tone:	Positive	Sad	Angry
Related words:			

Audience, Purpose and Tone

4) Write **two** sentences for each situation described below.
   Make sure your writing is appropriate for each audience and purpose.

   a) A leaflet advising people on how to stay safe at the beach.

   ....
   ....
   ....

   b) A letter to a prospective employer persuading them to hire you.

   ....
   ....
   ....

5) Write at least **four** sentences to suit the audience and purpose given below.

   Audience: landlord   Purpose: to inform

   ....
   ....
   ....
   ....
   ....
   ....

6) Write a short text on a separate page using your own chosen audience, purpose and tone.
   Swap with a partner — can you work out the audience, purpose and tone of their text?

Notes

Developing Sentences

Here's some extra practice with using joining words — they'll help you to develop your sentences.

1) Draw lines to match each bit of extra information to the sentence that it starts.

During the interview,	I filled my car up with petrol.
Before I drove to work,	I have learnt a lot about first aid.
Since becoming a lifeguard,	she asked me about my previous jobs.
After I finish work today,	it was a scam.
Although the email seemed real,	I am going to walk along the river.

2) Rewrite the two sentences in each box below as **one** full sentence. Use an appropriate **joining word** and a **comma**.

a) Remi needed some ingredients. He went to the supermarket.

....
....

b) Igor didn't wash the car. He did tidy the house.

....
....

c) Tilly might go shopping. Tilly might go to the park.

....
....

Developing Sentences

3) Read the debate below.

a) Write each joining word in the correct gap.

Therefore   and   but   because   However

Should Under 16s be Allowed Smartphones?

I believe that young people shouldn't own smartphones .... they can be harmful. Young people are more vulnerable to developing a screen addiction which can reduce their concentration, lessen their interest in other hobbies .... weaken their communication skills. Smartphones can also damage young people's well-being by increasing their exposure to cyberbulling. ...., improvements to security features are trying to tackle this. Other improvements are also aiming to make technology safer for young people to use, ... there's still a lot more that could be done. ...., in my opinion, the risks outweigh the benefits.

b) Write your own response to this debate.
Use the joining words 'while', 'until' and 'although'.

If you want to, you could write a longer answer on a separate sheet of paper.

....
....
....
....
....

Notes

Organisation and Structure

Now try these extra questions — they focus on the organisation and structure of your writing.

1) Write **two** sentences using each of the phrases below.

   a) for example

   ....
   ....

   b) for instance

   ....
   ....

   c) such as

   ....
   ....

2) Add the words below to the correct places to complete the recipe.

   Secondly   until   Firstly   Finally   then

   - ...., add 1 spoonful of oil to a large pan on a medium heat.

   - ...., add vegetables and stir-fry until they begin to soften.

   - Remove the vegetables from the pan and sauté diced garlic and ginger .... fragrant. Add the remaining ingredients for the sauce.

   - Return vegetables to pan, ... stir to coat them in the sauce.

   - ...., serve with rice or noodles.

Organisation and Structure

3) Read the text below from an article about a famous actor.
Insert **three** '//' symbols to show where new paragraphs should start.

> Helly Bell, an iconic actor known for her wit, remains a celebrated figure in film history.   Beyond her stunning performances in films like "The Fool" and "Dinner with March", Bell's dedication to helping young performers succeed has earned her phenomenal respect.   Born in Scotland in 1925, Bell's early life was impacted by the Second World War.   Despite those challenging teenage years, her passion for singing and acting led her to land roles in films that showcased her comedic talent.   Bell also devoted a lot of her adult life to helping disadvantaged children.   These days, Bell remains a recognisable figure — thousands of people pass the statue of her in her hometown every day.   Bell's dedication to helping young people and her unforgettable sense of humour continue to charm audiences globally, making her a true icon.

4) Write at least **six** sentences about what you do in your spare time.
Include at least **three** joining words and **three** paragraphs.

....
....
....
....
....
....
....
....
....
....

Notes

Communicating Clearly and Coherently

Here are even more questions — these are about communicating clearly and writing coherently.

1) Write a number in each box to put each part of this plan in a sensible order.

Hidden Disabilities	Title
I'd like to start by explaining what hidden disabilities are.	
In conclusion, I believe we need to increase awareness of hidden disabilities.	
For example, they might affect your mood, mobility or a combination of things.	
A hidden disability is defined as a physical or mental condition that isn't visible.	
There are many different types of hidden disabilities.	

2) Write down a supporting sentence for each of the opinions below.

   a) 'I'm glad she won the competition.'

   ....

   ....

   b) 'My favourite season is winter.'

   ....

   ....

3) The following text contains **five** spelling mistakes. Rewrite the text with the correct spellings.

   I would like to lern more about your start-up company. I recently worked on a project with Kirsty, who I beleve is one of your colleagues. She gave me your contact details and told me I shoud talk to you about my own busines plans. Let me now if you're interested in organising a meeting or a video call.

   ....

   ....

   ....

   ....

Communicating Clearly and Coherently

4) Rewrite the sentences below to communicate more clearly.

   a) Abdul wrote the report, then Abdul sent the report to Abdul's colleagues.

   ....

   ....

   b) I play football and I do badminton and I also play tennis and squash.

   ....

   ....

   c) Her car are parked in the car park, but the parking meter are broken.

   ....

   ....

5) 'Everyone should vote whenever they can.'
   Write at least **four** sentences giving your view on this statement.
   Include at least **two** opinions.

   Make sure your opinions are supported with a reason.

   ....

   ....

   ....

   ....

   ....

   ....

   ....

Notes

Format and Layout

These practice questions will help you get to grips with the structure of different types of texts.

1) Draw lines to match each letter feature to its location or purpose.

   Your address — Sign-off to use if you know the recipient's name.

   'Yours sincerely' — Use if you don't know the recipient's name.

   'Dear Sir / Madam' — Written in the top right corner.

   Recipient's address — Written above the letter on the left.

2) Using the prompts for newspaper articles below, write an engaging headline for each one.

   a) An article discussing the success of a local athlete.

   ....

   b) An article reporting on the discovery of a new species of plant.

   ....

   c) An article celebrating a summer carnival.

   ....

3) Anya has planned an email to persuade her colleagues to attend a team-building activity day. Read Anya's plan below.

   <u>Details</u>
   - What: Day at an adventure centre
   - When: May 15th — leave at 8 am, arrive by 10 am
   - Where: Skip and Leap Activity Centre (transport provided)

   <u>Anything else</u>
   - Bring comfortable shoes and a change of clothes in case it rains.
   - Food will be provided at the centre.

   On a separate sheet of paper, use the plan to write an email for Anya.

Format and Layout

4) Rewrite the following leaflet on a separate sheet of paper with a clearer layout. You should include at least **one subheading**, **paragraphs** and a **bullet point list**.

> Street Food Market
> Event details: 12 pm on 16th May at Flowerbill Park. Expect a delightful afternoon of tasting delicious food from over 20 different stalls. There will also be musical entertainment and children's activities. There's no need to RSVP. Please invite friends and family — everyone is welcome. Prices will vary at each stand and cash payments are preferred.

5) Your local council is hosting a discussion evening for residents in the area. Plan a report which:

- Gives information about positive events taking place in the local community.
- Explains a significant issue in your area.
- Suggests improvements that could be made.

Use the space below to plan your answer. Write your answer on a separate sheet of paper.

Notes

Language and Register

You've reached the final page of topic-based questions — these ones are all about language and register.

1) Rewrite the following sentences more formally.

   a) Hey Kevin — where've you been?

   ....

   b) Could you give me a sec, I'm on the phone.

   ....

   c) I'll be free from 6 pm, wanna grab some food?

   ....

2) Using the words provided, write **two** sentences persuading people to stop littering.

   discarded   consequences

   ....

   ....

3) Rewrite the following message to a hotel more formally.

   Hiya,
   I thought I'd message to see if you've got a room free over the August bank holiday?
   Basically, it's my birthday that week so it'd be neat if I could get a good deal or something.
   Ring me whenever you get a chance. See you later!
   Jack

   ....

   ....

   ....

   ....

Language and Register

4) Write each of the specialist words below in the correct box.
   There should be **two** words in each of the boxes.

   campaign   circulation   compensation   contents

   cyberspace   glossary   interest   nutrition

   qualifications   referee   software   volunteer

Reading	Technology	Health
....	....	....
....	....	....

Recruitment	Finance	Fund-raising
....	....	....
....	....	....

5) Using the prompts below, write a sentence that includes at least **one** specialist word.

   a) Starting a new job.

   ....
   ....

   b) Opening a new bank account.

   ....
   ....

Notes

Exam-style Practice

Functional Skills

English — Level 2 — Writing

Exam-style practice

Instructions to candidates:

- Have a go at these practice tasks, then ask your teacher to mark them.
- There are **nine** practice tasks in total.
- Before you start answering a task, read it carefully to make sure you understand it.
- You could make a brief plan for each task before you start writing.
- You will be assessed on your spelling, punctuation and grammar in each task.

Your assessment is likely to contain two tasks — you don't need to answer all of these practice tasks in one go.

1)

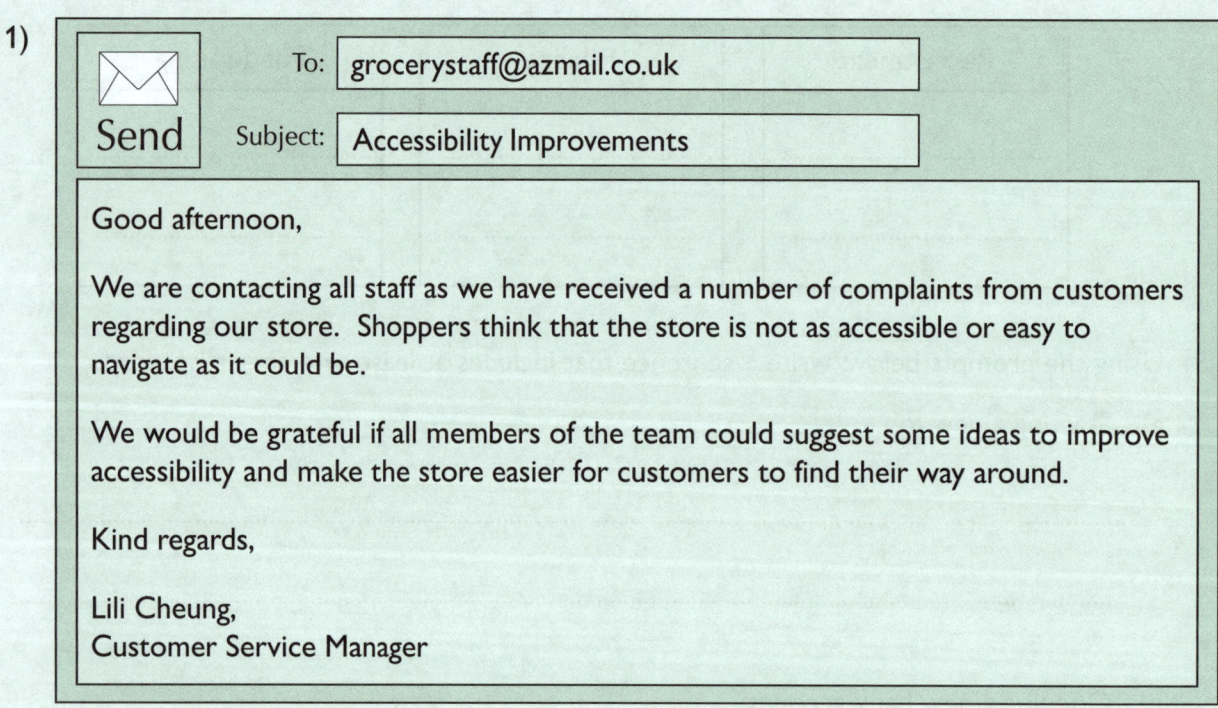

To: grocerystaff@azmail.co.uk
Subject: Accessibility Improvements

Good afternoon,

We are contacting all staff as we have received a number of complaints from customers regarding our store. Shoppers think that the store is not as accessible or easy to navigate as it could be.

We would be grateful if all members of the team could suggest some ideas to improve accessibility and make the store easier for customers to find their way around.

Kind regards,

Lili Cheung,
Customer Service Manager

Write an email to your manager with some suggestions to improve your workplace.

In your email, you should:

- describe any problems that you have seen
- explain how you think the store's layout can be improved
- persuade your manager to make your suggested changes.

Aim to write about 250 to 300 words.

Plan and write your answer on a separate sheet of paper.

Exam-style Practice

2) You have recently completed two different courses: one was an online course, and the other was classroom-based.

Write a blog about your experiences aimed at people who are about to start one of these courses. Your blog should persuade people to choose your preferred course.

In your blog post, you should:

- say what you liked or disliked about the courses
- explain any differences between the courses
- explain why other students should choose your preferred course.

Aim to write about 250 to 300 words.

Plan and write your answer on a separate sheet of paper.

3) **Appeal for witnesses following accident**

Raitown Police Service would like to speak to anyone who was near Fountain Street in Raitown at around 8 pm on Friday night. If you saw the accident, please use the online form to submit your eyewitness account and help us find out what happened.

Write an eyewitness account to submit to the Raiton Police Service.
In your account, you should:

- outline what you were doing at the time
- explain what you saw
- describe any important details.

Aim to write about 250 to 300 words.

Plan and write your answer on a separate sheet of paper.

Exam-style Practice

4)
> A local job centre is organising a careers fair at the library. It will be an opportunity for people to meet local employers and learn about different career options.
>
> The centre have asked you to create an advertisement that will be used to promote the event in the local area.

Write a leaflet informing people about the fair.

In your leaflet, you should:

- outline the details of the event
- explain why people should attend
- persuade people to attend the event.

Aim to write about 250 to 300 words.

Plan and write your answer on a separate sheet of paper.

5)

Tidal Trends
A New Sustainable Swimwear Brand for Ocean Lovers

Stay stylish and eco-conscious this summer in our new range of swimwear made completely out of plastics recovered from the ocean.

Why not visit our website to see our full range? You can also find us on social media.

You bought some swimsuits made of recycled plastic from Making Waves and were really happy with them.

Write a review about the products on an online fashion forum.

In your review, you should:

- describe the items you bought from Making Waves
- explain why you are happy with your purchase
- encourage people to support Making Waves.

Aim to write about 250 to 300 words.

Plan and write your answer on a separate sheet of paper.

Exam-style Practice

6)
>
>
> Dear Resident,
>
> We are excited to share that we are applying for permission to develop a new holiday resort on the outskirts of your town, and we want to hear from you! Local opinions are important to us as we plan this project.
>
> We are particularly interested in learning how you feel about this proposed development.
>
> Please let us know your thoughts by responding to this letter. More details on how to get in touch can be found on our website.
>
> Yours sincerely,
> A.B Holiday Resorts

Write a letter responding to A.B Holiday Resorts.

In your letter, you should:

- describe how the holiday resort might benefit your local area
- describe any problems the holiday resort might cause
- explain whether you think the new holiday resort is a good idea or not.

Aim to write about 250 to 300 words.

Plan and write your answer on a separate sheet of paper.

7) Write an article for the local newspaper about a community awards night you recently attended.

In your article, you should:

- describe the event and attendees
- explain what the awards were for and who won
- give your opinion of the night.

Aim to write about 250 to 300 words.

Plan and write your answer on a separate sheet of paper.

Exam-style Practice

8) You've just started a new job as a fitness instructor at a local gym. The management team want you to encourage more people to join the gym and take part in some of the new fitness classes on offer.

Write a leaflet encouraging people to do more exercise.

In your brochure, you should:

- explain why it's important to do regular exercise
- describe the gym and what people can do there
- encourage people to join the new fitness classes.

Aim to write about 250 to 300 words.

Plan and write your answer on a separate sheet of paper.

9) There are numerous events planned by your local council throughout the winter season. As a community volunteer, you've been asked to write an article informing people about these events. The organisers also need more volunteers, so have asked you to spread the word.

Event	Dates	Location
Indoor Markets	1st - 22nd Dec	Market Square
Winter Grotto	1st - 24th Dec	Pine Forest
Ice Rink	15th Nov - 15th Jan	Leisure Complex

Write a newspaper article informing people about the upcoming events.

In your article, you should:

- explain what events are happening
- persuade people to attend the events
- encourage people to volunteer at the events.

Aim to write about 250 to 300 words.

Plan and write your answer on a separate sheet of paper.

About the Test

It's good to be prepared — so here's all the information you'll need for the Level 2 English Writing Paper.

The Basics

The Writing component of Level 2 English is assessed with **one** test.

The format of your assessment depends on your exam board.

You might take this test on a **computer** (on screen) or on **paper**.

Your teacher should be able to tell you who your exam board is.

You'll likely have **one** or **two** writing tasks to complete:

- Tasks are usually based on **different scenarios** and **formats**. E.g. you might need to write a letter, article, email or report.
- You'll be expected to write around **200-300** words for each task.

Word counts are a rough guide — you don't need to count every word you write.

You will have **around 1 hour** to complete both tasks.

Read any tasks carefully and make a brief plan before you start writing.

If you have time, check your work when you've finished.

How Will I be Marked?

You'll need to demonstrate your writing skills across **both** writing tasks. You should:

- Use correct **spelling**, **punctuation** and **grammar**.
- Communicate **information**, **ideas** and **opinions** clearly.
- Write texts of a **suitable length** with enough **detail**.
- Use appropriate **formats** and **structures** in your writing
- Use **organisational markers** correctly.
- Adapt your **language** to match your **audience** and **purpose** (including using **persuasive techniques** and **specialist words**).
- Use **complex sentences** and **paragraphs** where appropriate.

You aren't allowed to use a dictionary during your writing assessment.

You need to show these skills consistently throughout the test — e.g. you need to use correct grammar throughout.

Jot down information about the test you're going to be sitting here.

Notes

Individual Learning Plan

After each lesson or topic, use the table below to record your progress. Then you and your teacher can identify what you still don't feel confident with, why you found it difficult and what you can do to improve.

1. What I Can Do Now	2. What I Found Hard
Example: I can use plurals correctly	Using prefixes and suffixes

Individual Learning Plan

Individual Learning Plan

If you want more space to write your plan, go to: cgpbooks.co.uk/fs-english or scan the QR code in the header to find a printable PDF of this table.

3. What I Need To Improve On	4. What I Will Do To Improve
Remembering spelling rules	Write a list of commonly misspelt words

Glossary

Advertisement (advert)	A text type that persuades the reader to do something, for example buy a product.
Alliteration	When words that are close together begin with the same sound.
Apostrophe	A punctuation mark that shows that letters in a word are missing, or that something belongs to someone.
Article (grammar)	Words used before nouns to show specificity.
Article (text)	A text type usually found in newspapers, magazines or online.
Audience	The person or people who read a text.
Blog	A text type found online, written about personal opinions and experiences.
Bullet points	A way of breaking up information into separate points in a list.
Conversational tone	Chatty writing style normally found in informal texts.
Descriptive writing	Writing that tells the reader what something is like.
Direct address	Writing that uses 'you' to address the reader directly.
Email	A text type written to a person, or group of people, which is sent online using an email service.
Emotive language	Language that appeals to the reader's feelings.
Explanatory writing	Writing that tells the reader about something.
Formal writing	A type of writing that sounds serious and professional.
Forum	A webpage where people discuss their opinions on a particular subject.
Impersonal writing	Writing that doesn't tell you anything about the writer's personality or opinions.
Informal writing	Writing that sounds chatty and friendly.
Instructive writing	Writing that tells the reader how to do something.

Glossary

Layout	How a text is presented on the page using different organisational features.
Leaflet	A text type, usually given away for free, that gives information about something.
Letter	A text type written to a person, or group of people, which is sent in the post.
Organisational features	Any part of the text which affects how the text looks, e.g. colour or bullet points.
Personal writing	Text that is written from the author's point of view and uses emotional language and opinions. It sounds like it's talking to the reader.
Persuasive writing	Writing that tries to convince the reader to do or feel something.
Prefixes	Letters added to the start of a word which change the word's meaning.
Purpose	The reason a text is written, e.g. to persuade or to explain.
Report	A text type that gives information about something that has happened or may happen.
Rule of three	A list of three words or phrases used to create emphasis.
Silent Letters	Letters which you can't hear when a word is said aloud, e.g. the 'k' in 'knife'.
Slogan	A short, memorable phrase used in advertising.
Specialist words	Words specific to particular subjects or contexts.
Style	The way a text is written, e.g. a text may be formal, informal, advisory or humorous.
Suffixes	Letters added to the end of a word which change the word's meaning.
Tense	Whether a verb is talking about an action in the past or the present.
Tone	The way a text sounds to the reader, for example personal or impersonal.
Verb	A doing or being word.
Webpage	A document located on the internet.

CGP

www.cgpbooks.co.uk

Name ....

Functional Skills

English: Speaking, Listening and Communicating

Level 2

Course Booklet

Answers available online

CGP Books — The Choice of Champions!

They know it... you know it... everyone knows it!

cgpbooks.co.uk

Contents

✓ Use the tick boxes to check off the topics you've completed.

Knowledge Organiser..2 ☐
Picking Out Information..4 ☐
Identify relevant information from
extended explanations or presentations.

Following Narratives and Arguments.....................6 ☐
Follow narratives and lines of argument.

Responding Effectively...8 ☐
Respond effectively to detailed or
extended questions and feedback.

Asking Questions..10 ☐
Make requests and ask detailed and pertinent questions
to obtain specific information in a range of contexts.

Communicating Clearly...12 ☐
Communicate information, ideas and opinions clearly and
effectively, providing further detail and development if required.

Expressing Opinions & Making Arguments.........14 ☐
Express opinions and arguments and support
them with relevant and persuasive evidence.

Choosing Your Words..16 ☐
Use language that is effective, accurate
and appropriate to context and situation.

Moving Discussions Forward..................................18 ☐
Make relevant and constructive
contributions to move discussion forward.

Knowing Your Audience..20 ☐
Adapt contributions to discussions to
suit audience, purpose and medium.

Being Heard and Staying Focused.........................22 ☐
Interject and redirect discussion using
appropriate language and register.

Practice Activities..24 ☐
About the Test..25 ☐

Free digital extras!

To get your extras, go to **cgpbooks.co.uk/fs-english** or scan the QR code below.

This will take you to:
An online answer booklet
Individual Learning Plan pages
A Knowledge Retriever

A QR code next to a 'Listen' stamp takes you to the audio player. You can access all the audio tracks and their transcripts by scanning these codes.

The audio tracks in this booklet are short examples. In your assessment, you will have to speak for a longer amount of time in a group of three or more people.

Published by CGP

Written by Rikki Ball

Reviewer: David Norden

Editors: Aimee Ashurst, Tom Carney, Polly Jackson, Alex Thompson

With thanks to Hannah Roscoe and Glenn Rogers for the proofreading.
With thanks to Beth Linnane for the copyright research.

Specification points in Contents contain public sector information licensed under the Open Government Licence v3.0. https://www.nationalarchives.gov.uk/doc/open-government-licence/version/3/

ISBN: 978 1 83774 211 0
Printed by Elanders Ltd, Newcastle upon Tyne.
Graphics from Corel®

Text, design, layout and original illustrations © Coordination Group Publications Ltd (CGP) 2025 All rights reserved.

Photocopying this book is not permitted, even if you have a CLA licence.
Extra copies are available from CGP with next day delivery • 0800 1712 712 • www.cgpbooks.co.uk

Knowledge Organiser

These pages contain the key info you need. They're great to refer to if you need to know what's what.

Picking Out Information

Listen out for:

- **Key points**
- **Examples**
- **Extra information**

- **Summarise** important information.
- Pay attention to **context**.
- **Don't** write **everything** down.

Following Narratives and Arguments

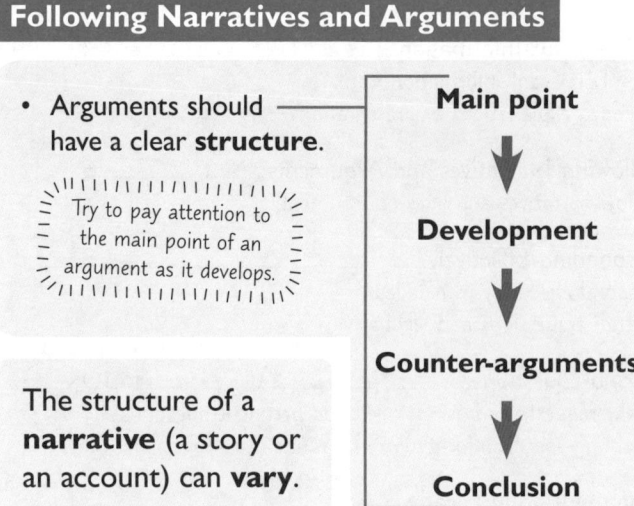

- Arguments should have a clear **structure**.

Try to pay attention to the main point of an argument as it develops.

The structure of a **narrative** (a story or an account) can **vary**.

Responding Effectively

- ✓ **Acknowledge** the speaker's point.
- ✓ Pay attention to **body language**.
- ✓ Keep a calm and respectful **tone**.
- ✓ Use facts and subject knowledge to provide **evidence** and **examples**.

- ✗ **Don't** interrupt impolitely.
- ✗ **Don't** be dismissive.
- ✗ **Don't** become defensive.
- ✗ **Don't** give incomplete answers.

If you have something to say, wait for a chance to speak.

"Your presentation was interesting but you could have included more evidence. How much did you research the topic?" → "Thank you for the suggestion, I will take that into account. I did do some research, and what I found was that..."

Asking Questions

Open questions:

"What are your plans for the weekend?"

- Need a **detailed** answer.
- Encourage more **discussion**.

Closed questions:

"Is your birthday party on Saturday?"

- Can be answered with **limited** responses.
- Often have a '**yes**' or '**no**' answer.

Your questions should be relevant to the information you want to find out.

Communicating Clearly

Make sure you **consider** your audience — give extra detail when it is **relevant**, but don't overwhelm them.

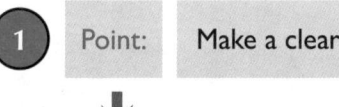 **Point:** Make a clear point.

 Evidence: Support your point using facts and relevant subject knowledge.

 Explanation: Explain how the evidence backs up your point.

Knowledge Organiser

Choosing Your Words

Your language should be:

Effective
- **Interest** and **engage** your audience.

Use adjectives and imagery to make your language more exciting.

Accurate
- Use **clear** and **precise** wording.
- Give examples.

Use a dictionary to check any words you aren't sure of.

Appropriate
- Your language should **match** your **audience**.
- Avoid slang.

Use formal language for a professional audience.

Expressing Opinions & Making Arguments

Opinion — *expresses a thought or feeling.*

- A personal belief — may not be factual.

Often start with "I think" or "I believe".

Argument — *presents evidence to persuade.*

- More likely to use facts and evidence.

May start with "Studies suggest" or "Experts say".

Moving Discussions Forwards

Stay on topic by:
- asking relevant questions
- building on other people's ideas

Be constructive by:
- giving relevant information
- suggesting solutions

Knowing Your Audience

You will need to adapt your speech depending on:

 Audience
Who you are communicating with.

You should speak formally in professional settings. You can speak less formally to friends.

 Purpose
Why you are communicating with them.

 Medium
How you are communicating with them.

A medium is a method of communication — e.g. a presentation or a discussion.

Being Heard & Staying Focused

To keep a discussion on track, you may have to...

Interject — *briefly interrupt.*
This is useful if:
- you need to add an important point
- someone is dominating the conversation

It's important to do both of these things **politely**.

Redirect — *guide people to a specific topic.*
This is useful if:
- the conversation is going off-topic
- the conversation is becoming repetitive

Picking Out Information

When you listen to someone speak, you need to be able to pick out the most important information.

Concentrate on What People are Saying

Do:
- ✓ Note down any **key points**.
- ✓ Summarise **important information**.

Don't:
- ✗ Write *everything* down.
- ✗ Ignore any **context**.

Now Try This

1) Draw lines to match each **term** below to the correct **definition**.

   Extra information — The overall argument being made.

   Example — Information that adds detail but is not necessary to understand the topic.

   Key point — Evidence that supports an argument.

2) The table below contains sentences from a speech about the benefits of classical music. Write each of the **terms** from Question 1 in the correct part of the table.

The Benefits of Classical Music	Term
Studies have shown that listening to classical music can improve academic performance.	
People have linked listening to other genres, such as rock music, with helping young people to express themselves.	
Listening to classical music can have many positive effects in various areas of your life.	

3) With a partner, take it in turns to briefly talk about a topic you care about. Pick out and note down the key points from each other's speeches.

Level 2 English: Speaking, Listening and Communicating

Picking Out Information

4) Listen to Hana's presentation about climate change.
   Pick out information from the speech and use it to fill in the table below.

Part of Speech	Notes
Topic	Climate Change and the Environment
Key Points	
Examples	
Extra Information	

Your notes don't need to be full sentences.

5) Write down **two** opinions Hana gives in her presentation.

   1 ....

   2 ....

Notes

Following Narratives and Arguments

An argument should be easy to follow — a good structure can help people understand your points.

You Should Practise Listening to Narratives and Arguments

Do:
- ✓ Pay attention to the main lines of argument.
- ✓ Look for supporting information.

Don't:
- ✗ Take information at face value.
- ✗ Ignore counter-arguments.

Arguments Should Have a Clear Structure

Narratives are stories or accounts: the structure can vary.

For example, an argument about renewable energy may look like this:

①	**Introduce the point**	Renewable energy is essential for sustainable development.
②	**Develop the idea**	Renewable energy reduces greenhouse gas emissions and dependence on fossil fuels.
③	**Consider counter-arguments**	Some say that renewable energy systems are expensive to set up, but they can save money in the long term.
④	**Conclusion**	Renewable energy is crucial for environmental and economic sustainability.

Now Try This

1) Put the correct word or phrase from the following list into each of the gaps below.

clear   narrative   line of argument   persuade

A .... is a structured account or representation of an event. It often involves the telling of a story, usually with a .... beginning, middle and end.

A .... is a sequence of statements, reasoning and evidence presented to support a viewpoint. It aims to .... an audience by building a compelling case to support its viewpoint.

Level 2 English: Speaking, Listening and Communicating

Following Narratives and Arguments

2) Listen to Nick talk about plant-based diets.
Fill out the table below by writing **two points** in each box.

Part of Speech	Notes	
Topic	Plant-based diets	*Remember: your notes don't have to be full sentences.*
Main Arguments		
Persuasive Evidence		
Counter-arguments		

3) Using Nick's presentation as a guide, fill out the table below to plan an argument on a topic of your choice. Write **one sentence** in each box.

Introduce the point:	
Develop the idea:	
Consider counter-arguments:	
Conclusion:	

With a **partner**, practise making your arguments to each other.
Were the four parts of the speech clear to identify when you listened to your partner?

Notes

Responding Effectively

Once you've finished making your argument, you should be ready to hear people's thoughts.

Be Prepared for Questions and Feedback

Do:
- ✓ Listen carefully
- ✓ Clarify understanding
- ✓ Stay calm and composed
- ✓ Address the key points
- ✓ Provide evidence and examples

Don't:
- ✗ Interrupt
- ✗ Ignore body language
- ✗ Become defensive
- ✗ Dismiss concerns
- ✗ Provide incomplete answers

You Should Respond to People Appropriately

What to do	Why
Acknowledge the speaker's point	This shows that you value the speaker's opinion and helps to move discussions forward.
Pay attention to your body language	Positive body language, like eye contact and smiling, can show that you are concentrating and make other people feel more comfortable.
Consider your tone	A respectful and calm tone can help people to take information in.
Use facts and subject knowledge	These support your response, making it seem more credible and persuasive.

Now Try This

1) Tick the boxes next to the scenarios below that show **helpful responses**.

   Luke asked Meg to repeat herself when he didn't understand the point she made. ☐

   Rebecca didn't make eye contact with Pranav when he was speaking. ☐

   Zuri agreed that David had a point, before suggesting another idea to him. ☐

   Milena raised her voice when Paula challenged the point she was making. ☐

   Joshua supported his response to Finn with evidence from his research. ☐

Responding Effectively

2) Find a partner. For each scenario below, one person should give the feedback and the other person should practise responding to it.

> **Scenario 1**: A team member is giving their team leader feedback about a recent project.
>
> **Feedback**: "I think the deadlines set for our last project were unrealistic and communication across our team needs improvement."

After each scenario, discuss your experience and think about how you could both improve.

> **Scenario 2**: An audience member is giving a speaker feedback about their presentation.
>
> **Feedback**: "I enjoyed your presentation, but I think you could have explained the main points more clearly."

> **Scenario 3**: A manager is giving feedback to another employee.
>
> **Feedback**: "You've done a great job recently, but I'd like to see you take more initiative in team projects. How can we support your growth?"

3) Listen to Luca's interview. Note down any ways that Luca **responds** to Mia **effectively**.

4) Name **one thing** Luca does that is inappropriate.

Notes

Asking Questions

You have to be comfortable listening to other people and asking questions to find out more information.

Ask Questions to Find Out More Information

Do:
- ✓ Be clear and specific.
- ✓ Ask open-ended questions.

Don't:
- ✗ Be vague.
- ✗ Make assumptions.

Questions can be Open or Closed

Make sure any questions you ask are **relevant** to the topic.

- **Open** questions need **detailed** responses and encourage **discussion**.
  E.g. *How do you see your future?*

- **Closed** questions can be answered with limited responses, usually **'yes'** or **'no'**.
  E.g. *Is it raining today?*

Now Try This

1) Use a **dictionary** to find the **definition** of the word 'pertinent'. Write what it means in the box below.

   You will be expected to ask pertinent questions in your speaking assessment.

2) Tick **one box** for each question below to show whether it is **open** or **closed**.

Question	Open	Closed
What motivates you to follow your current career path?		
Do you find it easy to access academic support?		
How do you manage your time between studying and social activities?		
Do you feel satisfied with the quality of your meal?		
Are you going to David's party tomorrow night?		

Level 2 English: Speaking, Listening and Communicating

Asking Questions

3) Draw lines to match each question word to its purpose.

Why		To find out a time
Where		To find out a reason
When		To find out a location

4) Change each closed question below into an open question. Ask a partner your questions.

   a) Would you like to visit Cornwall?

   ....

   b) Was this meeting helpful?

   ....

5) Listen to Sam's presentation. Write **three open questions** to ask Sam. Your questions should be as detailed as possible.

   1 ....

   ....

   2 ....

   ....

   3 ....

   ....

Notes

Communicating Clearly

Communication is key when it comes to your Speaking, Listening and Communicating exam.

Give Extra Detail When it's Helpful

Do:
- ✓ Consider your audience
- ✓ Be concise and focused
- ✓ Use supportive evidence

Don't:
- ✗ Be ambiguous
- ✗ Overwhelm the audience with information
- ✗ Interrupt or ignore feedback

Make Sure You Develop Your Ideas

One way of making sure you communicate clearly is to:

Make a **point** → Support it with **evidence** → **Explain** how the evidence backs up your point

'Wheels Up' is one of the best garages I've ever taken my car to.	Their prices are low and they explain everything very clearly to customers.	This brings the garage lots of business and customers always feel well-respected.

Now Try This

1) Draw lines to match each sentence below to either point, evidence or explanation.

- These various new developments show how fast technology advanced during the Victorian era.
- The Victorian era was a time of great change for many people.
- Victorian inventions included the light bulb, the telephone and the steam engine.

Point

Evidence

Explanation

2) Use the space below to note down some facts about your favourite sport.

Now **present** your information to a partner.

Remember to give examples and develop your points.

Communicating Clearly

3) Listen to Alex and Ali discuss financial literacy.
   Give **one piece of evidence** and **one explanation** for each point below.

Track 5

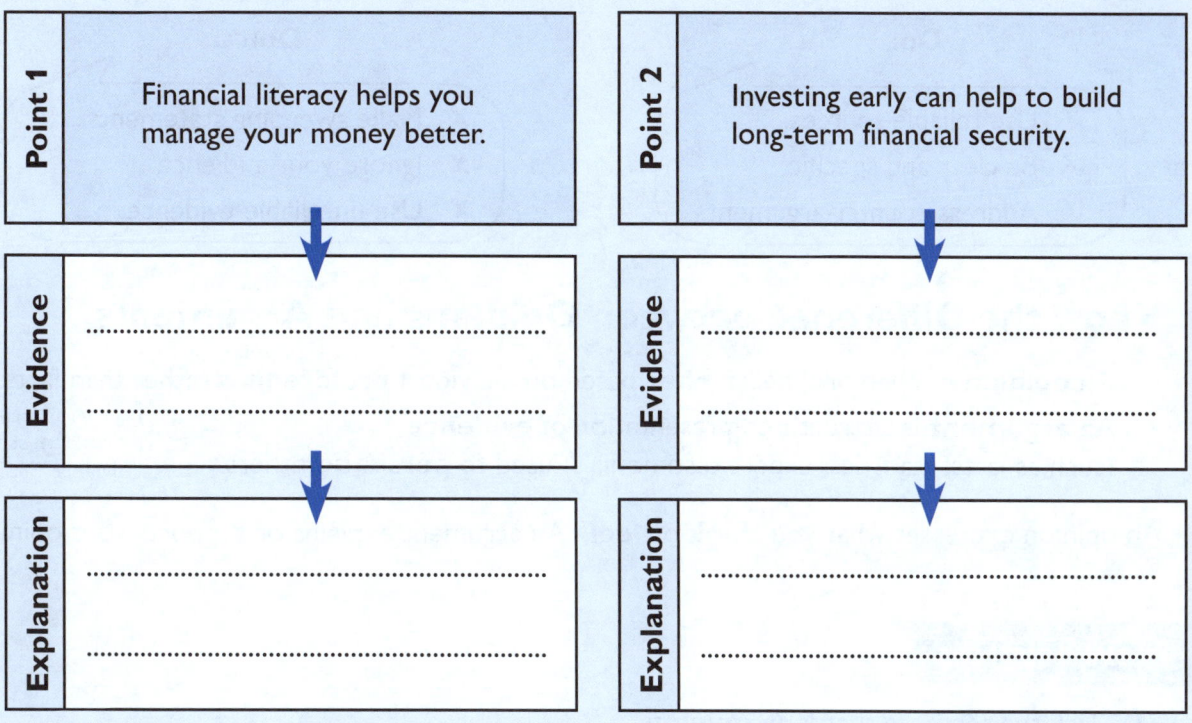

4) Use the space below to plan a short presentation on the importance of access to healthcare.

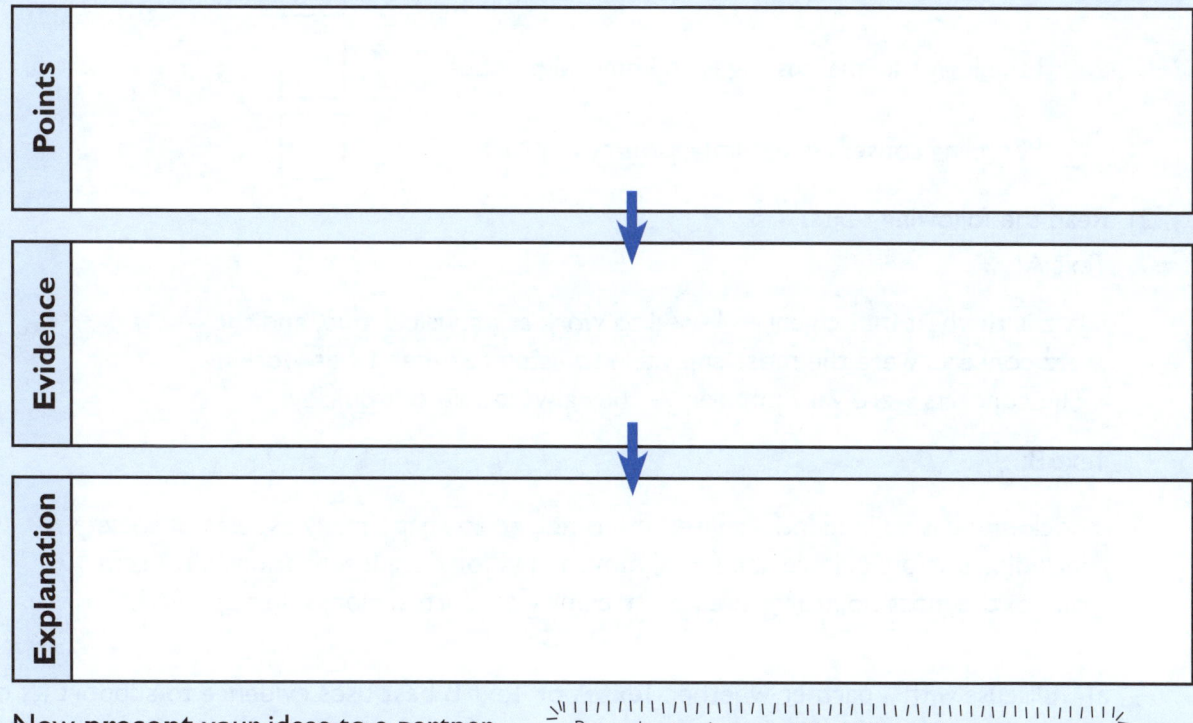

Now **present** your ideas to a partner.   Remember to give supporting details and develop your points.

Notes

Expressing Opinions & Making Arguments

A big part of communicating effectively is being able to express your opinions and arguments clearly.

Support Your Opinions and Arguments with Relevant Evidence

Do:
- ✓ Use reliable sources.
- ✓ Be clear and specific.
- ✓ Address counter-arguments.

Don't:
- ✗ Make sweeping statements.
- ✗ Ignore your audience.
- ✗ Use unreliable evidence.

Know the Difference between Opinions and Arguments

- An **opinion** is a personal belief, often based on individual **preferences** rather than facts.
- An **argument** is a structured presentation of **evidence** (such as facts, statistics, expert testimonials) used to **persuade** others.

Opinions often start with 'I think' or 'I believe'.

An opinion expresses what you **think** or **feel**. An argument explains or supports your opinion.

Now Try This

1) Tick the sentence that is an **opinion**.

   Office dress codes are used in many workplaces. ☐

   I think that animal testing is an immoral practice. ☐

   Recycling conserves natural resources. ☐

2) Read the following texts.

   Text A:

   > Jazz is the best music genre. I used to work at a music venue, and the jazz concerts were the most enjoyable to listen to when I was working. The concerts were very popular — they always sold out quickly.

   Text B:

   > Rock music is an influential genre. It has helped to shape many aspects of society including fashion, culture and social movements for decades. Rock also remains one of the most popular genres on streaming platforms, alongside pop music.

   a) Discuss with a partner whether Text A or Text B best uses evidence to support its claim.

   b) Circle the text you think best uses evidence. Give **one** reason for your answer.

   Text A / Text B ....

Expressing Opinions & Making Arguments

3) Listen to Sasha's presentation about remote working. *(Listen — Track 6)*

   a) Write down Sasha's main argument.

   ....

   b) What is Sasha's opinion on not commuting to the office?

   ....

   c) Which of the following does Sasha **not** use in her speech? Circle **one** option.

   A personal preference / A counter-argument / Another person's opinion

   d) Did you find Sasha's argument persuasive?   Yes ☐   No ☐

   e) Give **one** reason for your answer.

   ....

4) With a partner, each choose **one** of the following opinions.

   All cars should be electric.   **Art and science are equally important.**

   Research your chosen topic.
   Use the box below to write down any **persuasive evidence** you find in your research.

   Take it in turns to make a persuasive argument for your chosen opinion.

Notes

Choosing Your Words

Carefully selecting the words you use will help you to communicate your point to your audience.

Pay Attention to Your Word Choice

Do:
- ✓ Consider your audience.
- ✓ Be clear and precise.
- ✓ Adapt your language.

Don't:
- ✗ Use overly complicated language.
- ✗ Use slang or be too casual.
- ✗ Use an unfriendly tone.

Use Language That is Effective, Accurate and Appropriate

Effective:

Use engaging language to interest your audience.

E.g. The atmosphere at the athletics competition was **electric**.

Accurate:

Use the right words to express your point.

Be as **specific** as you can, and use **examples** if you have any.

Appropriate:

Adapt your language to suit your audience.

Always use **formal** language in a **professional** setting.

Now Try This

1) Tick the sentences below that are **appropriate** for a formal setting.

   Researchers have been looking into possible solutions. ☐

   I bet it's really tricky to dance professionally. ☐

   It's good to take some time to chill out in the evening. ☐

   We are currently reaching out to volunteers. ☐

   There is a variety of equipment at the sports centre. ☐

   It's usually best to use formal language unless you know who you're talking to personally.

2) Give **one** reason why the following phrase would **not** be appropriate in a formal setting:

   "Let's hang out later and have a chat about it."

   ....

Choosing Your Words

3) Imagine that you need to give a professional presentation on a new video game. With a partner, discuss how each sentence below could use more **appropriate** language. Record your ideas on the lines provided.

   a) Our mates are all dying to play the game.

   ....

   b) We've sorted all the weird bugs the last version of the game had.

   ....

   c) Check out this ace new feature we threw into one level.

   ....

4) Listen to Ali's presentation about healthy eating.

   a) Give **two** specific examples that Ali uses.

   1: ....

   2: ....

   b) Give **two** informal phrases that Ali uses.

   1: ....

   2: ....

   With a partner, discuss and suggest how these phrases could be made more formal.

   ....

   ....

Notes

Moving Discussions Forward

To keep a discussion moving forward, you need to make contributions that build on the conversation.

Conversations Usually Have a Purpose

Do:
- ✓ Stay on topic.
- ✓ Build on others' ideas.
- ✓ Ask relevant questions.

Don't:
- ✗ Get off-topic.
- ✗ Dominate the conversation.
- ✗ Give unhelpful criticism.

Your Contributions Should be Relevant and Constructive

Discussions often have a **goal** — e.g. to find out information, to ask for advice or to reach a decision. It's helpful to make contributions that **support** this goal.

- Ask **relevant questions** to get more specific information.
- Constructive contributions **add** to a discussion:

Your bus is often late. Would a more flexible start time help?
Providing feedback and offering a solution is constructive.

You're always late to work.
Only providing criticism is not constructive.

Now Try This

1) Your friend has asked for your advice on improving their piano playing.
   Tick **one** box to show whether each of the following contributions is constructive or not.

	Constructive	Unconstructive
a) "Your technique isn't very good."	☐	☐
b) "You could hire an experienced teacher."	☐	☐
c) "Have you tried watching other people play?"	☐	☐
d) "I'm not interested in music."	☐	☐

2) "We need to do something to reduce speeding in the local area."

   Tick the response that would best move this discussion forward.

   "People drive far too fast down the main road." ☐

   "Let's petition for a 20 mph speed limit." ☐

Moving Discussions Forward

3) Listen to the discussion between Moe, Hana, Mia and Sam.

   a) What is the goal of the discussion?

   ....

   b) Draw lines to show which phrases move the discussion forward and which don't.

   "You could join me at next week's class if you'd like?"

   "Have you ever been to the running club in the park?"

   "I have no idea. I don't take the bus there."

   Moves the discussion forward.

   Doesn't move the discussion forward.

   c) With a partner, talk about how any phrases that didn't move the discussion forward could be improved. Give **one** suggestion below.

   ....

   d) Which speaker dominated the conversation more than others? Underline **one** name.

   Moe   /   Hana   /   Mia   /   Sam

   Give **one** reason for your choice.

   ....

   Suggest **one** way this person could improve their communication skills.

   ....

4) In a small group, discuss **one** of the following statements:

   All towns and cities should have a library.

   Shopping online is more fun than shopping in person.

   Remember to keep your contributions relevant and constructive.

Notes

Level 2 English: Speaking, Listening and Communicating

Knowing Your Audience

You should change how you communicate to suit your audience and purpose — it's important to adapt.

Remember Who You Are Speaking to and Why

Do:
- ✓ Use suitable language.
- ✓ Adapt your tone.

Don't:
- ✗ Overuse slang or technical terms.
- ✗ Use the same tone all the time.

Make Sure You Know How to Adapt Your Speech

The language and tone you use should reflect:

- Your **audience** — who you are communicating with:

    "It's a pleasure to meet you."
    Speak formally in a professional setting.

    "Hey, it's great to see you."
    You can speak more casually to friends / family.

- Your **purpose** — the reason you are communicating ⟶ e.g. to explain or to inform.

- Your **medium** — how you are communicating ⟶ e.g. a presentation or a discussion.

Now Try This

1) For each of the following scenarios, tick whether you should speak formally or informally.

		Formal	Informal
a)	Giving a speech at a charity dinner.	☐	☐
b)	Having a discussion with your boss.	☐	☐
c)	Talking to a family member.	☐	☐
d)	Giving a presentation at work.	☐	☐

2) Match each of the following purposes to the medium that would better suit them.

Giving information to a large group

Sharing ideas with another person.

Explaining something to several people.

A presentation.

A discussion.

Knowing Your Audience

3) With a partner, discuss the language and medium that might best suit each scenario below. Record your thoughts on the lines provided.

You could also think about what tone you might use.

   a) You want to persuade a friend to try living more sustainably.

   Language: ....

   Medium: ....

   b) You're teaching a local business how to become more sustainable.

   Language: ....

   Medium: ....

4) Listen to Luca and Hana's presentation about job interviews. *(Listen — Track 9)*

   a) What is the **main purpose** of the talk?

   ....

   b) How would you describe the tone of the presentation? Tick **one** box

   Serious ☐   Encouraging ☐   Negative ☐   Humorous ☐

   Give **one** reason for your answer.

   ....

   c) Give **one** other way that Luca and Hana adapted their presentation for their purpose.

   ....

   d) With a partner, discuss any ways that you think the presentation might be adapted for each of the following audiences:

   College students applying for their first jobs.   **Experienced employees applying for promotions.**

Notes

Being Heard and Staying Focused

If a conversation starts to get off-track, you need to know how to steer it back in the right direction.

Sometimes You Need to Interrupt a Conversation

Do:
- ✓ Use respectful language.
- ✓ Be clear and confident.
- ✓ Acknowledge previous points.

Don't:
- ✗ Interrupt abruptly.
- ✗ Be impolite.
- ✗ Ignore or dismiss anyone.

Learn When to Interject or Redirect

Interjecting means briefly interrupting a conversation.
You may need to interject if:

- you have an **important** and **relevant** point to add. → If I could just interrupt a moment...

- one person is **dominating** the conversation. → Excuse me, but...

Redirecting means guiding a conversation to a specific topic.
You may need to redirect if:

- a conversation is getting **off-topic**. → To return to the original point...

- a conversation is becoming **repetitive**. → We could also consider...

People often need to redirect a conversation back to a previous topic.

Now Try This

1) Draw lines to show which interjections below are polite and which are impolite.

   "What do you think?"   **Polite**   "I'd like to point out that..."

   "I'm talking now."   **Impolite**   "To go back to your earlier point..."

2) Tick the phrase below that is the **more polite** way to redirect a conversation.

   "All that matters is picking a date for the event, so let's focus on that." ☐

   "I understand your concern about ticket costs, but let's pick a date first." ☐

   Give **one** reason for your answer.

   ....

Level 2 English: Speaking, Listening and Communicating © CGP — not to be photocopied

Being Heard and Staying Focused

3) Listen to the discussion between Sam, Sasha and Luca.

   a) Give **one** example of a polite redirection.

   ....

   b) Give **one** example of someone acknowledging another person's point.

   ....

   c) Which person interjected impolitely during the discussion? Tick **one** box.

   Sam ☐   Sasha ☐   Luca ☐

   Give **one** reason for your answer.

   ....

   Suggest **one** way that they could have interjected more politely.

   ....

4) In a small group, choose one of the following topics to discuss:

   | How important is public transport? | How do mobile phones affect social interaction? | How does music affect your mood? |

   a) Before you begin your discussion, pick **one** person in the group to try to steer the conversation off-track with unrelated interjections. Everyone else should try to keep the discussion focused on the topic.

   Everyone in the group should be polite and respectful at all times.

   b) Now choose a different person to make unrelated interjections and discuss one of the other two topics. Afterwards, talk about how the discussions went.

   Think about how you kept the conversation on track:
   - What was challenging?
   - Did you discover any helpful ways to interject or redirect?

Notes

Practice Activities

The activities below will give you a good idea of what your assessments will be like.

- There are **three** activities for you to practise.
  These activities will need to be done in **a group** of **three or more** people:

  | A formal discussion on an unknown topic. | A presentation on a chosen topic. | A question and answer session about a presentation. |

- You will need to demonstrate **all of the skills** covered in this booklet across the three activities.

  You can find a list of the assessment criteria on the next page.

Practice Activity 1

A **formal discussion** on an **unknown** topic.
Choose one of the topics below:

'unknown' means that you'll be expected to find or consider new information as part of this discussion.

- "The use of artificial intelligence in society or the workplace."
- "Taking care of the oceans."

Take some time to research the topic and plan your response.
Then **discuss** the topic with your group for up to **10 minutes**.

Practice Activity 2

A **presentation** on a topic of your choice.
You can use one of the suggestions below if you'd prefer.

- A local tourist attraction
- A hobby or interest
- A charity you support

Take some time to research your topic and plan your presentation.
Then give a **5-10 minute** presentation on it.

Practice Activity 3

A **question** and **answer** session about a **presentation**.
It could be your presentation or someone else's.

You could do practice activities 2 and 3 one after the other.

After listening to a presentation, **ask questions** and **discuss** it for **5-10 minutes**.
You should aim to:

- Ask relevant questions
- Make constructive contributions

If you gave the presentation, you should aim to:

- Answer questions clearly and with enough detail

About the Test

For Level 2 English, you'll complete assessments to show your skills. Here's all the information you need.

The Basics

The number of assessment tasks you'll have to complete and the amount of time you have to complete them depends on your **exam board**.

Your teacher should be able to tell you who your exam board is.

The assessment is usually carried out in a group of **three or more people**.

You'll likely have **two or three** different tasks to do, e.g.:

- A formal **discussion** with a small group on an unknown topic.

- An individual **presentation** on a topic of your choice.

- A **question-and-answer session** or **discussion** based on a presentation.

For each assessment, you should be told your topic several days in advance so you can prepare..

You should have **5** to **15 minutes** to complete each task. This does not include preparation time.

The audio tracks in this booklet are short examples for skill-based practice. You will have to speak for a longer time in your assessment tasks

How Will I be Marked?

You'll need to meet **ten** assessment criteria across **all** of your assessment tasks:

1) Pick out **relevant information** from other people's presentations or discussions.
2) Follow **narratives** and **arguments**.
3) **Respond** effectively to **questions** and **feedback**.
4) Ask **questions** that are clear and **relevant**.
5) Communicate your **ideas** and **opinions** clearly.
6) **Express opinions** and arguments and support them with **persuasive evidence**.
7) Use **effective**, **accurate** and **appropriate** language.
8) Make **constructive contributions** to discussions.
9) **Adapt** your **language** to suit your audience, purpose and medium.
10) **Interject** and **redirect** discussions in an appropriate manner.

You need to show these skills consistently throughout the tasks — you can't just ask one question to meet criteria number 4.

Notes

Jot down information about the test you're going to be sitting here.

CGP

www.cgpbooks.co.uk

Functional Skills

English

Level 2

This pack contains course booklets for each area of the Level 2 English qualification. The booklets have study notes and clear examples matched to each learning objective, with lots of questions and helpful knowledge organisers.

We've also included online audio recordings (with transcripts) for the Speaking, Listening and Communicating booklet, so you can practise responding to real conversations. Great stuff!

Unlock your Online Edition (including Answers)

This pack includes a **free Online Edition** containing all **three Course Booklets** and **full answers**. To access these digital extras, just scan the QR code below or go to **cgpbooks.co.uk/extras**, then enter this code!

2238 8206 6953 6734

By the way, this code only works for one person. If somebody else has used this book before you, they might have already claimed the code.

P.S. Don't miss out on our Study & Test Practice and 10-Minute Tests!

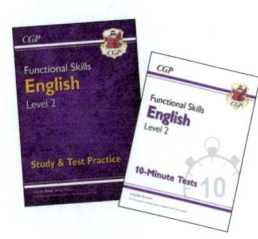